Penguin Masterstudies

Don Juan and Other Poems

Bernard Beatty read English with Philosophy at Birmingham University, where he gained his M.A. He has been lecturer in English at Liverpool University since 1964, Chairman of the Board of English at the same university since 1985 and Chairman of the English Association North since its inception in 1984.

He has published numerous articles, especially on Romantic literature, continuity in poetry, Dryden and Bunyan. He is author of *Byron's Don Juan* and co-editor of *Literature of the Romantic Period 1780–1830*.

He is married with four children, lives in Chester and is an amateur musician and choirmaster.

D1352332

Penguin Masterstudies
Joint Advisory Editors:
Stephen Coote and Bryan Loughrey

Byron

Don Juan *and Other Poems*

Bernard Beatty

Penguin Books

Penguin Books Ltd, Harmondsworth, Middlesex, England
Viking Penguin Inc., 40 West 23rd Street, New York, New York 10010, USA
Penguin Books Australia Ltd, Ringwood, Victoria, Australia
Penguin Books Canada Ltd, 2801 John Street, Markham, Ontario, Canada L3R 1B4
Penguin Books (NZ) Ltd, 182–190 Wairau Road, Auckland 10, New Zealand

First published 1987

Filmset in Monophoto Times
Made and printed in Great Britain by
Richard Clay Ltd, Bungay, Suffolk

Contents

appear, however, that many acquire either the habit or the ability to read poems with pleasure. Byron's best poems are of considerable length, yet we have progressively tended to squeeze long poems out of syllabuses and normal reading habits, replaced them by novels and kept only a small, token presence of short poems to represent 'poetry'. Nevertheless, we will get nowhere with Byron, or with English poetry as a whole, unless we learn to read and enjoy long poems. How can we do this?

We can begin our very brief answer to this question by emphasizing that poems should be read in different ways, as they themselves dictate. Most of Byron's poetry is best read rather more rapidly than that of Keats or Wordsworth, for instance. More of Byron's lines should be taken in at any single reading.

If we read Byron's verse steadily and quite briskly in this way, we will not always understand every line or phrase that he writes; however, we should not interrupt the flow of reading in order to correct this. On the other hand we should always read Byron's verse with the sense in mind and expect every line to make sense. This does not mean that we are faced by a string of simple assertions or that musical effects are unimportant, but that Byron despised obscurity in others and is rarely obscure himself. Energy and lucidity are the most obvious hallmarks of his writings. We should expect lucidity and make space for the scale of his energy.

Although we can make adequate sense of Byron's lines on a first reading in much the same way as we can make immediate sense of Chaucer's or Dryden's, it does not follow that we can grasp the whole sense and direction of a poem as we read it. The chief obstacles to coming to terms with Byron's poetry are the assumptions that poems are not intended to make sense at all or, that if they do make sense, this must be a fairly simple affair and confirm this or that view of the world. This is particularly relevant to Byron, because his poetry handles clichés, commonplaces and very large concerns all the time. We need to understand Byron's verse, therefore, as we read through it, but we should not be in a hurry to decide where Byron is in it himself or what it all adds up to.

When we read a conventional novel, we usually identify at an early stage with the main character in the story or with the voice and point of view of the narrator whom often we think of as the author. Once we have done this, we forget it and read the novel as though we were ourselves present within the world that it establishes. We call this 'getting into' a book and may be reluctant to carry on reading if we cannot 'get into' it. We never 'get into' poems in quite this way and this will be a main disincentive to reading them unless we can find a different kind of engrossment.

In fact, we work the other way round when reading poems. A long poem, such as Byron's *Don Juan*, will construct a world at least as vividly as any novel, but the words that set up this world remain in our consciousness as we read. We do not simply pass through them into the world described and forget that it is a work of Art rather than a slice of Life that we are immediately in touch with. When we read a poem, we not only see and hear a world in front of us, we remain conscious of what we are doing. Although we may be deeply moved as we read, we never transfer ourselves wholly into the world that so engages us. It is this position, always on the threshold of a world made out of words, which is the main source of pleasure in poetry; and, once the secret of this is discovered, we will find no other reading experience to match it.

The most important step here, therefore, is to register the words of a poem as we read them. The simplest way of doing this is to read them aloud. It is probably impossible to learn how to hear poetry internally unless, at some stage, we have put some effort into reading poetry aloud. We will not want to do any of this. It goes against the grain of our ordinary reading habits, seems eccentric and alarmingly increases the time it will take to read a poem. Unless we do so, however, we will never find out what poetry can do, never associate it with pleasure, and we will try to reassure ourselves that poetry is for other people because we are tone-deaf to it.

If, for instance, we read in this way one of Byron's shorter long poems such as *Parisina*, which is an excellent and comparatively easy poem to begin with, we will notice certain habits of voice and patterns of rhythm that are peculiar to it. Our first job is simply to register these as attentively as we can and not allow them to slip away from us. In doing so, we will find ourselves paying more or less equal attention to every part of the poem. This is extremely important. When we read, or more usually scan, a newspaper article with our eyes alone, we select the most important words and passages from it and use the rest simply as a rapidly discarded context to place the 'gist' that we have already isolated. We transfer these reading habits to novels and especially to poems, with disastrous consequences. Our eyes will often detect lines in poetry that seem to carry little or no significance and we assume that we need not register them at all. We should not be too punctilious about this, of course. It is not the case that every word and every line matters in every poem written. What we should not do is let our eyes tell us which the important lines are before we have actually read them with proper attention. The same rule applies to silence. Reading aloud forces us to use our lungs and make regular pauses to take in more breath. These pauses are used for musical and emotive effects in poetry and must always be registered even, indeed especially, in silent reading. For example, look at these typical lines wrenched out of context from *Parisina*:

> There whispers a voice through the rustling leaves,
> And her blush returns, and her bosom heaves:
> A moment more – and they shall meet –
> 'Tis past – her Lover's at her feet.
>
> And what unto them is the world beside,
> With all its change of time and tide?
>
> (2–3)

What do we see if, as advised, we 'look at' these lines? Surely very little. There are no apparent complexities or obscurities to detain us. The language is simple and we may be irritated by the repetition of 'and', obvious rhymes and extreme generality ('her', 'they', 'her Lover's', 'them', 'the world', 'time and tide'). This is, we presume, an important and intense moment when two lovers meet, but we are given no protracted description of interior feeling or external circumstance to help us to acknowledge this. By the standards of novel writing this seems to be thin, inexact language and, put alongside a metaphysical, or modern short poem, will seem to be clichéd and lacking in density.

Now let us try to read these lines, rather than merely look at them. We will need to mark the rhythm confidently. The first line should be said fairly rapidly in a whisper, with only the most momentary check at 'voice' but a slight lingering on 'leaves'. The next line is said more assertively, with a strong pause after 'returns' and 'heaves'. This is occasioned both by the meaning and the rhythm, for we have got used to a basic rhythm, based on three-syllable units ('through the rust[ling]', 'And her blush'), but 'returns' and '[bos]om heaves' leave us with more time than we need to say them. This, in effect, is continued into the next two lines, where the space made available by the two-syllable groupings is marked by dashes and pauses.

The effect of these adjustments in rhythm is to give us a sense of excitement, onrush and expectancy in the first two lines and then register the sudden stop and change as the lovers meet and freeze in a held posture. This is followed by a considerable pause that takes us across to a new section in the poem. The generalized language ('her Lover's at her feet') is entirely appropriate, for the lovers are seen as intense and representative embodiments of a passionate encounter that everyone can recognize. We are not interested in what is particular about this assignation (though the lady's 'blush' here involves, in context, a particular kind of guilt); on the contrary the next two lines generalize this occasion to the maximum possible extent. The lovers, held in this pause of verse, are set against the world and all manner of elemental change ('of time and tide'). The articulacy lies with the speaker here. The lovers themselves are in a speechless intensity that we guess at through the blank space and silence marked for our attention. Even this articulacy is not as straightforward as it seems. The line

> And what unto them is the world beside,

is breaking back into the three-syllable groups ('unto them', 'is the world'). We are close to the rapture of the lovers in their detached superiority to the world in these speeded-up lines. In the next line, however,

> With all its change of time and tide?

our attention is momentarily on the world and its mutability. There is a note of bitterness in this line, measured and held back into two-syllable units again, which implies that the lovers may not be able to sustain their rapturous indifference to the world indefinitely. They are marked out both for admiration and pity. The voice that asks the question, 'And what unto them . . .?' is quite different from that found in the excitement of the first two lines and the restrained factuality of the following two.

This account could be continued further, but enough has, perhaps, been said to demonstrate that change of voice, change of rhythm and the interposition of silence are crucial to the direct, emotional effects of these deceptively plain lines. These effects may appear complicated when set out like this, but they are not intended to be scrutinized separately and should make themselves felt in any proper reading. They will, however, disappear altogether if these lines are simply scanned with the eye for their 'gist' or some respectably complex 'image' to puzzle over.

An earlier point is worth re-emphasizing here. If there was not once a

18

person called Lord Byron who was, as he claimed, 'blood, bone, marrow, passion, feeling', then these effects would not exist. However, we should not jump to the conclusion that Byron is more present in the poignancy of 'And what unto them' or the bitterness of 'With all its change' than he is in the first four lines or, even, in the silences that he so exactly calculates. Sense and feeling must be registered immediately in verse like this, though we must allow Byron time to assemble the whole poem before we can say what it is doing and what it is ultimately concerned with. Most of Byron's poems work like this and should be read in this way.

Parisina is a good place to begin, because it is a narrative of an obviously dramatic kind and thus we are more inclined to stand back and watch its progression. Or rather, as in the lines quoted, we seem to be very close to the whispered voice of the lover as he brushes 'through the rustling leaves' and, at the same time, to be observing it all from an immense distance where we are also conscious of the endless changes 'of time and tide'. These effects of juxtaposed perspective are common in poetry, and Byron's poems are especially rich in them. We must, for instance, read reflective poems like *Childe Harold's Pilgrimage* or the digressive passages in *Don Juan* and *Beppo* in a similar fashion to the narrative and dramatic poems. We should not assume that reflective passages necessarily come more directly from Byron himself than the narrative episodes and that, consequently, we can identify these or those lines as an authorial viewpoint. On the other hand we must avoid the opposite error, which is to decide that Byron has no purpose in his poetry other than to present a series of irreconcilable views of the world. This is a better mistake to make, but it is still a mistake. Byron loved paradoxes, distrusted ready-made systems of thought and was keenly aware of the inconsistencies of human behaviour. He had a remarkable capacity for sympathy with different individuals and situations. But he did not think it impossible to praise virtue, castigate vice or recommend one path rather than another, and he always sought some resolution of the profound dilemmas that his verse proposes.

This is praise indeed, but, on the whole, Byron deserves it. He is a great poet and should always be taken seriously even when he appears flippant or mannered. Two kinds of misrepresentation are, unfortunately, still operative here and may interfere with reading him. The first is a distrust of the more obviously Romantic voice of Byron. There are strong elements of theatricality in *Childe Harold*, *Manfred* and other poems, and there are some passages that may seem offensive to common sense and egalitarian preference. For example, these lines from *Childe Harold* recommend unfashionably elitist territory:

> He who ascends to mountain-tops, shall find
> The loftiest peaks most wrapt in clouds and snow;
> He who surpasses or subdues mankind,
> Must look down on the hate of those below.
> Though high *above* the Sun of Glory glow,
> And far *beneath* the Earth and Ocean spread,
> *Round* him are icy rocks, and loudly blow
> Contending tempests on his naked head,
>
> (III, 45)

Similarly, Manfred is something of a Superman who despises the 'thoughts of men' and seeks out 'The difficult air of the iced mountain's top'. We can say at once that there are many passages in Byron's poetry that ridicule such Promethean superiority to ordinary life and that, even in *Childe Harold* and *Manfred*, we are not asked simply to endorse viewpoints like these. However, we cannot altogether dispose of the problem in this way. Non-egalitarian thoughts and feelings exist throughout literature and cannot be excised from our consideration. Even the most egalitarian movements celebrate their Lenins as well as their Long Marches. We need not assume that the extraordinary, the difficult and, to that extent, the superior are unsuitable objects of literary attention. In Byron's case too there is undoubtedly a link between his attraction to 'difficult air' and his unusually firm hold on the familiar patterns of life. In the few lines from *Parisina* looked at above, for instance, it is evident that there is, simultaneously, a sense of the unusual intensity of the meeting of these lovers set apart from 'the world beside' and a sense of the predictable, almost routine, character of their experience.

There are many great novelists, such as Scott, Dickens, Tolstoy, John Cowper Powys, D. H. Lawrence or Evelyn Waugh, who make us see ordinary reality as inseparable from heightened and extraordinary perspectives. Most novelists, however, simply confirm the widespread assumption that social, historical and natural worlds have little or no resonance in themselves except as the backdrop to, or opponent of, individual lives. Individual life is here some kind of vantage-point that we may shape a little for ourselves and peer out from on to a larger world that we cannot enter, explore or fully comprehend. Approaching Byron's long poems with these expectations is useless. When Byron looks at the familiar and everyday world, he does so with 'The difficult

air of the iced mountain's top' still in his being. He enters more fully into
that familiar world in his poetry and in his life than most of us, but
retains always that sense of oddity, precariousness, blankness, danger
and wonder that marks the one who stands 'with naked head' buffeted
by 'contending tempests' on 'The loftiest peaks'. There is no ordinary
world for Byron that can be separated from the baffling and mysterious
energies, bright and dark, which give rise to it. This double perspective is
the characteristic occasion of Byron's poetry and the resultant in-
congruity is the occasion of his outbursts of laughter. Here we come
across the second misrepresentation.

The poems of Byron that are most frequently read – *Don Juan*, *Beppo*,
The Vision of Judgement – were written after *Childe Harold*, *Manfred*
and the Oriental tales, and seem to repudiate Byron's earlier style and
conviction. In the first canto of *Don Juan* the narrator remarks ruefully
that he can

> ... feel no more the spirit to retort. I
> Have spent my life, both interest and principal,
> And deem not, what I deemed, my soul invincible.
>
> (I, 213)

If we put these lines against a famous passage from *Childe Harold* written
a year earlier, we find a different idiom and a different conviction.

> But I have lived, and have not lived in vain:
> My mind may lose its force, my blood its fire,
> And my frame perish even in conquering pain;
> But there is that within me which shall tire
> Torture and Time, and breathe when I expire;
>
> (IV, 137)

In *Don Juan* Byron appears to repudiate invincibility and in *Childe
Harold* appears to claim it. The obvious conclusion is that Byron changed
his mind as he grew older and rejected his earlier exalted opinion. There
is some truth in this, though it is not as simple as it seems. The point is
such an important one that we will keep approaching it from various
perspectives in this study. In particular we must not assume that Byron
has, as it were, let us off the hook so that we need not take his 'Romantic'
poems seriously and can take for granted that his best poems cut things
down to manageable sizes. In *Don Juan* alone the apocalyptic resonances
of the shipwreck in Canto II, Juan and Haidée's walk between land and
ocean bathed in the light of the setting sun, and the transcendent figure

21

of Aurora Raby in Cantos XV and XVI provide us with spectacles as exalted as anything in *Childe Harold* or *Manfred*. The chatty narrator of the lines quoted from *Don Juan* may have spent his life, 'both interest and principal', but he is just as convinced as the author of *Childe Harold* that there is something in him 'which shall tire/Torture and Time'. He is quite correct in this. It is the idiom and the reference points that have changed.

Byron himself is partly responsible for this second misrepresentation. He is self-conscious, ironical and anxious not to be wholly identified with any of the feelings and assertions that he delivers with such force. This is not because he has no centre of his own. On the contrary he is, as the narrator of *Don Juan* puts it,

> Changeable too, yet somehow *idem semper*;
> (*Don Juan*, XVII, 11)

'*Idem semper*' means 'always the same', and there is something constant in Byron, recognized by his friends, which allows him to make clear political interventions and to develop his ideas coherently. Nevertheless this constancy is rooted in his own recognition of the 'Changeable too'. He writes indignantly in his 'Letter on Bowles's Strictures on Pope' about Bowles's claim to have established 'invariable principles of poetry', exclaiming, 'I do hate that word "*invariable*". What is there of *human*, be it poetry, philosophy, wit, wisdom, science, power, glory, mind, matter, life, or death, which is "*invariable*"?' Byron knows too that the energy which shapes a strong assertion or powerful feeling is often used up in its own articulation and will then flow in the opposite direction. Hence the most truthful thing to do is to show how this occurs in history, how energies and counter-energies have wrestled with one another and formed some kind of resolution in real events. Fiction held, as Byron always held it, to the contrarieties of the self and the conflicts of history can tell the truth more fully than all the various political and intellectual systems, conventional or revolutionary, that deal only in tidied-up formulas abstracted from the flow of occurrences. Byron is deeply attached to the notion that poetry is only valuable in so far as it tells the truth, for, as he writes in the same public letter, 'If the essence of poetry must be a *lie*, throw it to the dogs.'

Similarly, Byron's sense of the theatrical form of private emotions and public life comes from a recognition of the inescapably stylized character of strong feelings and major conflicts. Those caught up in these things assert and find their selves in dramatic postures, emblematic tableaux and eloquent outbursts, but they also remain separated from these spectacles in some part of their being and thus resemble actors. Both the irony of *Don Juan* and the elegiac outbursts and sudden shifts of feeling in *Childe Harold* come from the same source. They are not necessarily contradictory modes.

It is for this reason that there are fewer quotations from Byron's letters in this study than might be expected. Although there are many pithy and illuminating comments to be found there, the danger is that anything Byron says in prose is likely to be taken as 'the truth' or what he 'really thought' about this or that. Byron's letters are not deceptions, but they are always intended for particular recipients and are adjusted accordingly. His most celebrated ones (to Murray his publisher but intended to be read to a small circle) are a very particular kind of performance where he is most anxious to dazzle his audience and to protect himself. He does both brilliantly. Byron is particularly skilful at allowing his immediate consciousness to flow in an apparently unedited fashion on to the page while, in fact, monitoring it in such a way as to hide much of himself from the reader. In a poem like *Don Juan* we get both this and a narrative which, together, give us far more of Byron than all his letters put together. It is a mistake, in the present writer's view, to refer to Byron's letters as though they are a more reliable guide to Byron's purposes in his poems than the poems themselves.

The last point only repeats what has been insisted on throughout this introduction: that we cannot readily separate fact and fiction in Byron. His extraordinary life has always claimed attention because it is both circumstantial and fabulous. His poetry, romantic or burlesque, always sets its sights upon the realm of fact. He is more at home with long poems than anything else, because long poems, unlike lyrics, shape out a large space where we find many things very familiar to us alongside unfamiliar objects and forms.

It is not hard to read Byron. All the signs are that *Don Juan* is the most accessible long poem in English and that much of Byron's idiom, view of poetry and subject-matter is now, in some ways, more immediately attractive to English readers who encounter him for the first time than at any period since the decline of his extraordinary reputation at the beginning of the nineteenth century. The difficulty is that we do not have a literary or moral vocabulary that will quite fit him, and so he is often pigeon-holed as a Romantic rhetorician, a satirist and a liberal who approved of sex and disliked war. These labels are not wholly false, but they are crass and ease us away from that ability to register and probe the contrariety of things that is the source of Byron's splendour, profundity and charm.

Lyric Poems

Some of the reasons why Byron excels in long poems and some recommendations as to how to approach these have been set out above. He did actually write many excellent short poems as well; these are still read but rarely studied. There are four important groups here. The earliest of these is usually called the 'Thyrza' poems after their designatee, who was, in fact, a choir boy whom Byron had known in Cambridge. Byron discreetly changed 'his' to 'her' in some of these elegiac poems. A later collection called *Hebrew Melodies* (1815) is mostly based on Old Testament situations and was designed to be set to music. An entirely different group called *Domestic Pieces*, addressed mainly to his wife and half-sister, is closely connected with the separation from his wife in 1816. Finally, there are some poems written in Greece, many of which were destroyed after his death; this was probably because they documented the struggle within Byron between his infatuation for a Greek youth and his determination to subordinate everything to the public cause that he had undertaken. Three of these lyrics survive and they are impressive. The most famous of them is 'On This Day I Complete My Thirty-sixth Year'. Many other lyrics written independently are worth reading, especially 'Prometheus' and 'So, We'll Go No More A-roving'. There remains 'When We Two Parted', printed below, which we will briefly discuss as fairly representative of Byron's lyric voice.

> When we two parted
>   In silence and tears,
> Half broken-hearted
>   To sever for years,
> Pale grew thy cheek and cold,
>   Colder thy kiss;
> Truly that hour foretold
>   Sorrow to this.
>
> The dew of the morning
>   Sunk chill on my brow –

It felt like the warning
  Of what I feel now.
Thy vows are all broken,
  And light is thy fame:
I hear thy name spoken,
  And share in its shame.

They name thee before me,
  A knell to mine ear;
A shudder comes o'er me –
  Why wert thou so dear?
They know not I knew thee,
  Who knew thee too well: –
Long, long shall I rue thee,
  Too deeply to tell.

In secret we met –
  In silence I grieve,
That thy heart could forget,
  Thy spirit deceive.
If I should meet thee
  After long years,
How should I greet thee?
  With silence and tears.

The first thing we notice about this poem is its rhythm. Many of Byron's lyrics, apart from *Hebrew Melodies*, have musical reference or direction. Some, for example, are called 'Stanzas for Music'. Here the rhythm is insistent, unusual, and is responsible for major effects. We read the poem in groups of two short lines which, together, make up the rhythm at the end of each second line, as indicated by the parentheses:

<pre>
  /   x   x   / x
When we two parted
 x /   x   x   /
In silence and tears, (xx)
</pre>

The rhythm marked here (/ marks stressed syllables, x marks un-stressed ones) does not appear to make any regular pattern if we look at the lines separately. If, however, we look at the regular occurrence of one stressed and two unstressed syllables (/xx) across both lines, then we see that there are three such groupings plus one final stress unaccounted for. I have added two unstressed syllables in parentheses here, which makes up the pattern. This can be done because the pause at the end of the second line exactly corresponds to two unstressed syllables. There is, therefore, a grouping of four similar units altogether. These metrical units are traditionally called dactyllic (/xx). They are the norm in the first stanza of 'When We Two Parted' and in the last four lines of the final stanza. This rhythm is quite unlike that of customary speech. This can be seen clearly in the stress pattern of the previous sentence set out below:

x / x x / x / / x / x /x /
This rhythm is quite unlike that of customary speech.

As this example shows, English rhythm is almost always rising (x/ or xx/) rather than falling. Most English speech and prose is like this. The beginning and end of Byron's lyric set up exactly the opposite cadence, which is why the rhythm is so obtrusive. In the rest of the poem, however, the stress pattern is reversed (xx/) to a more normal, though still galloping, rhythm. There is less space between the lines, because the unstressed syllables fall differently:

x / x x / x
The dew of the morning

x / x x /
Sunk chill on my brow – (x)

x / x x / x
It felt like the warning

Returning to the opening rhythm of the poem in its last lines gives a musical sense of closure but also unites the occasion of the remembered parting and the imagined future parting. This is ironical and emotive, because the feelings on the two occasions, and therefore the cause of 'silence and tears', are quite different. Silence, tears and rhythm are identical but on the first occasion they signal the inappropriateness of any other sign to a meeting that heralds severance. On the imagined second occasion, however, silence and tears now indicate the bitterness felt by one at the forgetting and deceit of the other. A similar effect is engineered metrically by the opening of the last stanza:

In secret we met –
In silence I grieve,

The first line lacks its customary weak syllable at the end and thus upsets the regular cadence. It mimics in this way the sudden cutting off of 'we met'. In general, the poem plays off silence and the rush of the speaker's volubility against one another to maximum effect much as in the extract from *Parisina* examined earlier.

The regular rhythm is heavily reliant upon obliging monosyllables and a bald, conventional vocabulary ('dew', 'fame', 'vows', 'knell', 'rue', 'spirit'). Both rhythm and diction suggest an impersonal poetic voice. Against this there is unmistakable personal tension that seems to threaten the mannered accomplishment of the verse, as in the second line below:

> They know not I knew thee,
> Who *knew* thee *too well*: –

> [my italics]

It is this exquisite balance of lightness, social grace, musical accomplishment and emotional urgency (compounded of nostalgia and bitterness) that gives the poem its force and makes it instantly recognizable as Byron's. He never attempts to do more than this in a poem of this length, which is why he rarely features in practical critical exercises. His lyrics remain quoted, however. Once read, this short poem is never forgotten. It is harder to describe such lightness of touch – Shakespeare's songs present us with a similar problem – than it is to set free-association rolling or to unearth laboriously the 'depth' that lies beneath the 'surface' of a poem. With most of Byron's lyrics it is to the surface, as to the sound of a song, that we must attend.

1. Tales and Satires

Beppo and Byron's Tales

(*The first section gives some account of Byron's tales in general but uses three of them,* The Corsair, Parisina *and* The Island, *as extended examples. The second section is entirely devoted to* Beppo.)

The Tales

Throughout his life Byron wrote narratives of some kind. He only used the word 'tale' of his first three stories and, later, regretted that he had used the term at all. It has stuck, however, especially to the group of verse narratives written between 1812 and 1816 (*The Giaour, The Corsair, Lara, The Bride of Abydos, The Siege of Corinth* and *Parisina*). Though written at the peak of Byron's 'London fame', they are, for the most part, based on memories of his time in Greece and Turkey (1810–11). For this reason the first five are often called 'Oriental' tales, though Byron said that the country of *Lara* was 'the Moon'!

There are four later narratives written in Switzerland or Italy. Each is quite distinct in character. These are *The Prisoner of Chillon* (1816), *Beppo* (1818), *Mazeppa* (1819) and *The Island* (1823). When we take note of Byron's eight experiments in dramatic narrative, his two dramatic monologues and add *Don Juan*, which can be seen as a sequence of seven tales, then the range of Byron's story-telling in verse is matched only, if at all, by Chaucer's. We will use the term 'tales' here for all Byron's narratives except *Don Juan* and the dramas.

Some features are common to all Byron's tales. Precise location is extremely important in them. Landscapes, costumes and customs are described with gusto and fidelity. A whole society is suggested, whether it be bourgeois, feudal or outlaw in character. This society is caught up in their action. Several depict warfare. All have some political motif.

Most of the tales are dominated by the psychology of the 'Byronic hero'. The Byronic hero is formed by a strange blend of Byron's outlaw heroes, parts of his own celebrated personality, and a whole series of semi-mythical and literary predecessors, including Milton's Satan. The early tales, together with *Childe Harold's Pilgrimage* and *Manfred*, established the Byronic hero as a European phenomenon that still has reverberations today. The later tales, however, especially *Beppo* and *The Island*, though still featuring this character-study, reduce its status and place it in a comic perspective. In the same way, and for the same reasons, the balance between dominant men and passive women is reversed in the later narratives.

All the tales are concerned with love, though they are not simply about love. In most of them love comes up against something irreversible that seems to be as much inside as outside human will. It is an ancient dispute whether human beings control their own actions or whether their social environment, upbringing or heredity control them. Theologically this is the argument about grace and free will; in secular thought it is about the rival claims of nature and nurture. More than most, Byron allows for the apparently innate human disposition towards evil expressed in the biblical story of the Fall of Man; yet at the same time he insists that his heroes choose their action and fate. It is said of one of them in *Lara*:

> Till he at last confounded good and ill,
> And half mistook for fate the acts of will:
>
> (I, 18)

This Macbeth-like fixity of purpose in a consciousness that insists on its own freedom fascinated Byron, but his heroes are marked too by a curious softness of heart. Conrad in *The Corsair* notes

> He marvell'd how his heart could seem so soft.
> Fire in his glance, and wildness in his breast,
> He feels of all his former self possest;
>
> (I, 16)

It is indeed this combination of unalterable defiance and sensitivity of heart, to women especially, that gives the Byronic hero his distinct character and makes him into so potent a European myth. It is this same combination that consistently causes his downfall. He is too proud to live purely within the confines of human love, but his softness of heart undermines his separate powers of action just when he has most need of them.

THE CORSAIR

The Corsair, for instance, opens with a description of Conrad, a kind of pirate chief, who, like most Byronic heroes, has settled into a life of crime because of some past social wrong done to him. He is

> Doom'd by his very virtues for a dupe,
> (I, 10)

He is mysterious, proud, guilty and apart:

> Lone, wild, and strange, he stood alike exempt
> From all affection and from all contempt;
> (I, 11)

Nevertheless he is prey to 'a softer feeling' for Medora, who lives a life wholly devoted to his presence, or rather to the memory of his presence, in a tower on their Greek island. At the beginning of the poem he goes to say farewell to her.

All this may seem a little silly, an early nineteenth-century pop video, but, like the latter, their relationship and its setting are not presented in a naturalistic way, as they might be in a novel or film. Everything is exaggerated, simplified and stylized, like an opera or ballet, in order to dramatize a series of oppositions. The important things to register in this opening section are the set-apart character of Conrad and Medora's love, and Conrad's refusal to commit himself wholly to this separate world. Medora complains that Conrad 'flies from love and languishes for strife' (I, 14). The word 'languishes', as the American critic Jerome McGann points out, is transferred cleverly from the realm of love to that of conflict. It is as though Conrad fears that he might repress his instinct for strife if he stays within the love-tower. Their leave-taking, which thus typifies their relationship, is given a clearly ominous character.

The middle section of the poem concerns Conrad's raid on a Turkish town, his capture, imprisonment and escape. The narrative here, like that of an adventure story, depends upon rapid changes of fortune and vivid incidents, but once again it has what we would call an 'emblematic' character. Conrad loses the fight for the burning town because, by his insistence on rescuing the harem women, he loses the initiative. He is betrayed, then, by his softness of temperament. Conrad is himself rescued from torture and death, on the other hand, by Gulnare, a Turkish woman whom he has saved from incineration. Gulnare rebels against her role as a 'toy' of her 'dotard' husband, the Pasha of the town, and murders her husband while he sleeps in order to ensure Conrad's escape. Conrad reacts with horror and revulsion to this desecration of 'softer feeling'. We find ourselves confused, for, clearly, Medora and Gulnare are complementary women. Each has what the other lacks, but Conrad can neither stay in Medora's haven of refuge nor accept Gulnare's complicity in crime. He is condemned both by the hardness and softness of his heart. When Conrad returns to his island home, in the final section of the poem, Medora is mysteriously dead in her tower. Again, we do not expect any naturalistic explanation for this. Conrad, equally mysteriously, leaves the island for ever and the poem ends.

The Corsair is typical of these early tales. It is powerful, sometimes crude and often brilliant in its narrative fluency and dramatized psychology. Each section of the poem, taken on its own, could easily be patronized by the modern reader (and by some modern critics). We could dismiss Conrad and Medora as flimsy male and female stereotypes, deride the adventure-story element in its central action and scorn the balletic pathos of Medora's unexplained death, but, by and large, we would be wrong to do so. Taken together, these episodes set up a complex interaction of male and female, individual and social, political and elemental forces. Conrad's impossible conflict between love's private world and the public world of action is a major theme across the centuries, found, for instance, in Virgil's *Aeneid*, medieval romance, Spenser's *Faerie Queene*, Shakespeare's *Antony and Cleopatra*, Tolstoy's *Anna Karenina* and D. H. Lawrence's *Women in Love*. We should respond in a simple way, however, to the glamour and energy of the setting. The sea, for example, is realized with wonderful force in many of the early tales.

We should also note the way in which every possibility in *The Corsair* – staying on Medora's isle, leaving it, living in society or out of it, fortitude or softness of heart, passive or active womanhood – is rendered impossible or fruitless. This world may be glamorous, but it is also bleak and vigorous in its hopelessness. This double sense of the beauty of sea and island, and the aridity of human life in this seeming paradise, is crucial to Byron's perception and the life of his verse. The psychology of the Byronic hero, alive and active, while simultaneously bored and at a dead-end, represents this clearly to us. Byron, like Wordsworth, is intensely interested in what it feels like to live on with stricken vitality in circumstances that are absolutely intolerable. Unlike Wordsworth, Byron characteristically associates this with the psychology of hell and damnation, with sexual energies and with problems of justice.

PARISINA

We see all these elements in the best of his Romantic tales, *Parisina* (1816). *Parisina* lacks the narrative invention and elemental energy of a tale like *The Corsair*, but it is compact, tightly structured and bright with intelligence. The story itself is simple and based on an anecdote that Byron found in Gibbon's *Antiquities of the House of Brunswick*, which he quotes in his Advertisement to the poem.

> Under the reign of Nicholas III. Ferrara was polluted with a domestic tragedy. By the testimony of a maid, and his own observation, the Marquis of Este discovered the incestuous loves of his wife Parisina, and Hugo his bastard son, a beautiful and valiant youth. They were beheaded in the castle by the sentence of a father and husband, who published his shame, and survived their execution.

Byron alters these circumstances in two details. One of these is minor. He changes the name of Nicholas to Azo, 'as more metrical'. His tale keeps to the tripartite division of Gibbon's account – (1) discovery (2) beheading (3) Azo's survival – but Byron deliberately exempts Parisina from the public execution of the lovers. Why does he do this? He wants to make Parisina's end more mysterious, so that we do not quite know what happens to her. Byron's narratives often tantalize us by not giving the reader sufficient information to know and understand everything that occurs. This is a trick of narrative to create interest and suggest horror, although Byron also uses it, above all in *Manfred*, to demonstrate the incompleteness of human knowledge in general and of the hidden web of connections that controls human lives. In *Parisina* Byron wants also to avoid too much concentration on the lovers themselves and to isolate the spectacle of Hugo's death so that he can challenge his father's justice. In each of these three sections Byron manipulates the reactions of the reader. At first we identify briefly with the rapturous intensity of the lovers. Then we are made aware of the guilt inherent in their simultaneous deception of Parisina's husband and Hugo's father. Our sympathy turns to Azo as he learns of their betrayal, but, after sentence of death is passed on Hugo, the latter upbraids his father in a magnificent tirade. He reveals that Azo has betrayed and abandoned Hugo's mother after seducing her and that Parisina was originally destined to marry Hugo but Azo taunted his own son with his illegitimacy. This places all the events that we thought we had understood in a different perspective. Instead of being a pathetic tale of guilty lovers doomed to a harsh but righteous death, it now looks more like a political fable which shows that justice is administered solely in the interests of a corrupt ruling class. Political resonances are invariably present in Byron's tales. Here they are very close to the surface.

This effect is heightened by Hugo's public admission of his guilt, calm acceptance of execution for his public crime and religious absolution for his private sin. This public clarity and peace in Hugo's consciousness is contrasted with the confined consciousness of Parisina, which is over-charged to the point of madness and, finally, with that of Azo. Azo's survival is the biggest surprise of the poem and a deeply Byronic one. We could never have anticipated at the beginning of the tale that it would conclude with a sympathetic sense of the final intensity of Azo's experience. His consciousness is now that of the Byronic hero:

> A mind all dead to scorn or praise,
> A heart which shunn'd itself – and yet
> That would not yield, nor could forget,
> Which, when it least appear'd to melt,
> Intensely thought, intensely felt:
> (*Parisina*, 548–52)

As if to underline and complete this strange reversal, the poem concludes with a striking image of Azo as a vigorous tree now blasted by lightning and leafless. This recalls the opening lines of the poem, which were full of a wonderful sense of the soft, lush foliage and gentle winds that pressed in sympathetically upon the lovers' assignation. Azo's intense inner life now seems more horribly vital than that of the two lovers.

The narrative skills here are evident and exemplary. What are they used for? Much as in *The Corsair*, the reader is continually trying to find a clear point of view. Is the love of Parisina and Hugo right or wrong? Good in itself, perhaps, but it contravenes social taboos and personal loyalties. Is Azo right to punish the lovers? Some punishment is due for their offence, but Azo is as guilty as they and there is a dreadful blurring of public and private motives in this judgement. Even the onlookers are caught up in these uncertainties. On the one hand they are ordin-ary moral beings who act like a jury, while on the other they are supine, treacherous and connive at public injustice. It is wrong to break the laws of God and men, yet those who uphold them are hypocrites and receive their own punishment. We can neither live by the law nor ignore it.

Punishment is central to Byron's conception here. Many of Byron's Romantic contemporaries produced fables in which, after transgression, punishment is evaded. Remorse or forgiveness or some vague idealism fend off the punishment due to crime. Hence there is little Romantic tragedy. Goethe's Faust goes to a vague heaven, not a definite hell. Coleridge's Ancient Mariner exists in some limbo midway between punishment and forgiveness. In Byron's fable, and it is typical of his relentlessness, all are punished. Parisina goes mad and loses Hugo; Hugo is executed; Azo lives on in hell. Why is this so?

Human reason dislikes the idea of punishment. Punishment seems to belong to the world of childhood, to deny the possibility of human change for the better and to simplify moral situations. In addition, as we saw in *Parisina*, those who carry out punishment must claim a righteousness that they are unlikely to possess. Byron keenly understood all this and lets Hugo say it for us. Later he wrote a play *Cain* (1821), which is entirely about this problem. In *Cain* punishment means, at first, expulsion from Eden after the Fall. In other words the everyday condition of human life is a form of punishment. Cain, like Hugo, protests at this apparent injustice, but, in the process of doing so, kills his brother, Abel. He thus brings death into the world for the first time and, ironically, himself completes the punishment caused by the Fall of his parents. At the end of the play Cain finds his punishment to be living on with the knowledge of what he has done, just as Azo must at the end of *Parisina*. Byron's fables suggest, then, that there is some gap between what our reason tells us about punishment and what actually occurs. The whole pattern of connection cannot be made transparent; punishment carries some meaning that reason cannot fathom. Indeed, punishment seems to make available to us, as nothing else can, the mysterious and specific character of human existence. We receive punishment as some sort of visitation beyond our scope of understanding and yet, somehow, we are wholly responsible for it ourselves.

These are the themes of Greek tragedy and of biblical history, but they receive a Byronic twist. Byron is interested in the intensity of suffering consciousness and with the strange vitality that it promotes. *Manfred*, is the most sustained presentation of this. (Emily Brontë, strongly influenced by Byron, clearly based the patterns of *Wuthering Heights* on the same theme.) The viewpoint we have been describing is a grim one. It was suggested in Byron's lifetime that he had reinvented the notion of hell and made people take it seriously just when 'enlightened' eighteenth-century thought had disposed of such barbarous notions. Yet much of Byron's poetry is anything but grim. It is exuberantly in love with life, hilarious, relaxed and tender. Although these things are opposites, Byron convinces us that in their depths they are connected, almost identical:

> While life's strange principle will often lie
> Deepest in those who long the most to die.
> (*Don Juan*, IV, 11)

Greek and Shakespearian tragedy seem to produce the answering viewpoint of comedy. We cannot have one without the other. Crucifixion and Resurrection form parts of a single meaning. Human beings do not have any deeper understanding than this. Byron's poetry rediscovers these unsayable connections and gains its unstoppable energies from them. It is not a matter, then, of Byron turning away from one to the other. It is true that he becomes more and more concerned with comic viewpoints as he grows older, but this is a different way of handling the same problems with which his early poems are concerned. *The Island* (1823) is the last of Byron's tales and of particular relevance because it puts together both tragic and comic perspectives in a single poem. Less austere than *Parisina*, it reverts to the elaborate settings and narrative intricacies of *The Corsair*. Although the most complex and ambitious of all Byron's tales, it is structured so cleverly and thought out so clearly that it is not difficult to understand.

THE ISLAND

The story Byron tells is based on the mutiny on the *Bounty*. In Byron's version the mutineers, led by Christian Fletcher, take possession of Bligh's ship in the South Seas, set Bligh and those loyal to him adrift in a longboat, and then return to the island of Toobonai (based on Tahiti), which, to them, represents paradise. In fact, some escaped to further islands and others were eventually caught and brought to trial. In Byron's tale one sailor (Torquil) is allowed to survive on Toobonai and the rest are caught or die in the fight to retake them. Though the poem was based on fairly recent fact, the island of Byron's poem belongs as much to myth and imagination as to history.

Throughout the eighteenth century there had been growing speculation as to what human beings would be like if removed from the inherited customs of European civilization. Some famous thinkers, such as Jean-Jacques Rousseau, speculated that human beings would be quite different and wholly better if they lived in a state of nature, and that mankind was enslaved, not improved, by social customs and laws. Was it not preferable to be a 'noble savage' rather than a tame citizen? As more and more 'primitive' people were discovered in the South Seas Islands or in North America, they were looked at and written about in order to confirm that they were happier and less wicked than Europeans (hence proving the new theories to be right) or, on the contrary, to support the older view that all human beings were tainted by the Fall of man and the laws of civilization were therefore a necessary corrective to anarchy. William Golding's novel *Lord of the Flies* is a recent island fable designed, it seems, to support the second view. Byron's *The Island* allows us to hold both views and this is the purpose of his poem. How does Byron get away with this paradox?

Literature, and especially poetry, is often commended nowadays because, unlike a book of scientific facts, it offers as many points of view as there are readers. There is some truth in this but not much. Byron, undoubtedly, would have hated such sloppy confidence and his poem gives subtle but definite answers to the very difficult questions that it raises.

The mutineers want to leave Bligh's ship and return to Toobonai (that is to say, human beings dislike the tyranny of law and order). We find always:

> The wish – which ages have not yet subdued
> In man – to have no master save his mood;
>
> (I, 2)

Sexual instinct is particularly important here. Customary life is founded upon countless acts of self-repression, but sexuality incites us to instant pleasure and seems to suggest that any repression interferes with the proper flow of natural life. So the mutineers disobey and rebel, then lay claim to an island paradise of leisure, natural appetite and sexual pleasure. Are they right to do so? Byron's poem gives a clearly negative reply.

The wrongness of the mutineers is shown in two ways. Firstly, the mutineers are punished, just like Parisina and Hugo. What they want is not right in the simplest sense. It does not work out. Secondly, the path they carve out for themselves back to paradise has conspiracy and crime as its starting point. They cannot wipe this out in their consciousness. Thus they live (especially Christian Fletcher) within the memory of past crime and the fear of future punishment. Although they may look as if they are in paradise, they are not and cannot obliterate their own awareness of boredom and guilt. Christian Fletcher ends up as the last Byronic hero. His defiant suicide, though magnificently realized in the poem, is not presented sympathetically.

It is therefore clear that we cannot switch to some simpler world where we all make love and not war, escape from a dark European history and live in untroubled fruitfulness. Byron intends us to reject the return to paradise, but of course Captain Bligh, though treated respectfully, is not the real hero of Byron's poem. Indeed, his tale allows and encourages us to imagine what it would be like to live in a natural paradise for ever. Hence he writes two ends into a single poem. Fletcher and his band die, but Torquil is allowed to escape from the naval search-party and to follow his lover, Neuha, in a fearful dive into the sea from which he does not, apparently, return. The pursuing sailors think that he has drowned or that something supernatural has perhaps occurred. In fact, he has followed Neuha down under the waves and up into the centre of a hollow rock that rises out of the 'unsympathetic flow' of the ocean. There he stays in safety, enjoying the light and food that she has brought with her, and also enjoying her while the threatening ship returns back to civilization. Torquil and Neuha are finally received back on to the island for ever in a great feast that concludes the poem.

In play here are all kinds of blatant sexual and religious symbols, which were as obvious to Byron, I think, as they are to us. Byron's purpose is, indeed, to make deep, common fantasies seem real and yet remind us that they belong to the imagination rather than to realized political life. His intention is not to nullify them or recommend a reactionary *status quo*. After all, Byron himself was about to leave Italy and his mistress a few months after writing *The Island* and join in the political struggle to free Greece from Turkish oppression. What he wants us to do is to balance very finely the necessary restraints of civilization (seen in Bligh's ship), the corruption of all political motives including revolutionary idealism such as Christian Fletcher's, and our deep longing for happiness, harmony between the sexes and oneness with natural life. We cannot base a view of life, or our actions, on any one of these. We have to hold them steadily together and reconcile, so far as we can, what we habitually imagine with what we habitually do. Poetry itself, as Byron sees it, is a particularly important means of reconciling sober understanding with visionary power.

There are all kinds of things wrong with *The Island*. While some of the verse is magnificent, some lines are inept. Nevertheless the conception and balance of the poem are profoundly impressive. We have had to simplify its patterns in this brief summary of Byron's tales, though we can now give a fuller account of one of the most interesting of them.

Beppo: A Venetian Story

PLACING THE POEM

Beppo (1818) is a comic tale quite different in character from Byron's Oriental tales such as *The Corsair*, although the key to understanding it properly lies in them. In many ways it reverses all their emphases, but in others it develops or modifies their characteristic features, or places them in a context where they further comic resolutions rather than dramatic intensities.

The Oriental tales, as we have seen, depend upon an exotic location, an exaggerated psychology and bursts of action that lead to death or intensify the guilty isolation of the survivor. The tales therefore locate value in intensity and in extreme situations. The manner of their narration, however, seems to undermine this intensity, particularly if we compare them with the hushed density and stillness of Keats's narrative poems, such as 'The Eve of St Agnes' or 'Isabella'. Byron's tales appear slapdash in comparison. Keats looks like an entranced craftsman, while Byron poses as a man of the world knocking out couplets while shaving.

The comparison with Keats will mislead us, however. The intensity that Byron is after is bound up with the rapidity of his verse. The poet appears to be improvising his words in the face of directly perceived characters and action. The artist is not hidden behind the poem like Keats but is exposed to us. This is not to say that there is no artistry in these tales. Byron can, for example, skilfully suggest various intermediate points of view belonging to other observers of the action or to major characters themselves. But it is the rapidity with which we are moved from description to psychology to action that is the most striking formal characteristic of these early tales, as well as the main cause of their infelicities. We are invited to respond to them at a first hearing and find ourselves caught up in the bravura of the poet who seems to improvise and expand them as we listen. *The Island* is more thoughtfully structured than this and *Beppo* seems quite different again.

The most obvious difference is the appearance in *Beppo* of a narrator who spends more time chatting about this and that than telling the tale. *Don Juan* is written in much the same way (see pp. 69, 71–3, 107–15), though *The Vision of Judgement*, written in the same stanza form and idiom, does not have a significant narrator. However, two things need to be stressed at the outset. The narrator in *Beppo* serves purposes specific to this particular poem and he is, in fact, fashioned out of the story-telling methods of the early tales.

Both these things need emphasizing, for *Beppo*, *The Vision of Judgement* and *Don Juan* have too often been lumped together as though they are all written in an identical way and should be seen as simply repudiating Byron's earlier practice. Of course there is some truth in this. In a letter to Thomas Moore Byron himself described *Don Juan* as written 'in the style and manner of *Beppo*' (19 September 1819). The mode of all three poems also owes a great deal to the contemporary comic poem *Whistlecraft* by John Hookham Frere, which Byron read immediately before writing *Beppo*. (For a fuller discussion of the stanza form used in *Beppo*, *The Vision of Judgement* and *Don Juan* see pp. 74–5, 115–22.) In addition Byron was influenced by his growing acquaintance with Italian poetry, which often mingled tones and moods in ways not habitual in English verse. Without these things, and Byron's own new experience of Italian life, *Beppo* would not have been written as it was. It still strikes the present reader, like it did Byron's contemporaries, as something fresh and new.

If we stand back a little, however, the development of Byron's tales from *The Giaour* (1813) to *The Island* (1823) is, very broadly, from horror to comedy. *Beppo* is pivotal in this broad pattern. The comedy does not consist in looking at something different from the horror but in looking at the same thing in a different way. For instance, the next tale that Byron writes, *Mazeppa* (written 1818, published 1819), describes the punishment that Mazeppa receives for making love to the young wife of a Polish count. He is strapped naked to the back of a wild horse that rushes out into wild and desolate countryside. There follows a magnificently vital account of Mazeppa's intermittent consciousness as he is forced to experience everything that the horse does as it crosses an icy river or, for a time, joins a wild herd. In a way, of course, the ride symbolizes the untamed passions for which Mazeppa is being punished, and the subject-matter of the tale – illicit passion, punishment and revenge – is the staple concern of all Byron's tales. Nevertheless these intensities are contained by a comic framework. The horse dies but Mazeppa is rescued and, in some strange way, his wild pride seems to have died with the horse that bore him. Now a cheerful old man, he tells the tale to Charles XII – a proud, conquering king fleeing from present defeat and therefore a suitable recipient for the moral of Mazeppa's story – but the king falls asleep during the tale. In these ways, though intensity and passion still form the centre of interest, *Mazeppa* appears to recommend acceptance, good humour and comic trust in events. *The Island*, as we have seen, similarly enfolds a tale of crime, revenge and death in another comic tale of love-trial and final happiness.

If we set *Beppo* within this sequence then and recall Byron's continual experiments in verse form, it is clear that his Venetian tale is part of a single pattern of development. The digressing narrator is an alternative way of conveying immediacy, authenticity and rapid fluctuations of reference to that developed in the Oriental tales. He is an alternative way too of representing masculinity and this is a useful way to begin our reading of the poem.

BEPPO: MASCULINITY AND FEMININITY

Though *Beppo* was published anonymously, the narrator is transparently George Gordon, Lord Byron, an aristocratic English poet who has newly taken up residence in Venice and is fascinated by its ways. But the narrator is also a device within the poem, a persona created by the poet for specific purposes. (For a more extended discussion of the role of the narrator, see pp. 49–50.) The narrator's masculinity plays an important part in these purposes.

Venetian life in *Beppo* is dominated by women. Men are wholly subservient, for the most part gladly so, to this domination. The voice of the narrator, however, exists as a separate realm in temporary independence from female rule. Nevertheless the purpose of this separate realm is primarily to celebrate women. Thus Byron implies that ancient Greek art, Italian painting, sculpture, drama, even Shakespeare's tragedies, exist as part of Man's celebration of Woman (see stanzas 11, 12, 15, 17, 46). The implication here is that all art is like this, though of course Byron knows that it is not and says so elsewhere. Though this may be so, the narrator's mode is that of a man talking to men. He invites his readers, for instance

> ... to bid their cook, or wife, or friend,
> Walk or ride to the Strand, ...
>
> (8)

Furthermore, when the narrator does assume a feminine manner to suggest his heroine's consciousness, we notice the difference immediately:

> One has false curls, another too much paint,
> A third – where did she buy that frightful turban?
> (66)

As we read the poem, therefore, we encounter a woman-dominated society that is mediated to us via a self-assured male poise. In the Oriental tales we are held by a similarly strong sense of the demarcation between male and female perceptions, but men dominate them and insist on a separate world of action of their own. Instead of these doomed Byronic heroes with shadowy female partners, *Beppo* represents a male world largely through the narrator's racy, man-of-the-world conversation that converts the rapid immediacy of Byron's earlier tales into a different use. It transforms too their normally passive heroines into the dominant forces in Venetian life.

However, the tale that the narrator tells us presents two other men who force us to modify these valuations. The tale itself is of the briefest. Laura, a pretty Venetian woman, is married to Beppo, a sailor-cum-merchant who, like Conrad in *The Corsair*, unaccountably does not return from a voyage. Laura, though upset, after a decent interval, unlike Medora, fixes herself up in the Venetian manner with a permanent liaison with a count. Half a dozen years later Beppo returns in the midst of a Venetian masquerade attended by Laura and her lover but, instead of a duel, Beppo and the Count eventually become good friends and all live fairly happily ever after.

Laura's Count represents men insofar as they wholly give themselves over to a feminine world and do not languish, as Byronic heroes usually do, after independence and 'strife'. The poem, for the most part, endorses this female supremacy, but the Count is supposed to trouble us a little. Though he is a man of taste and judgement, his acute discrimination between good and bad singers, dancers and musicians (31–3) is much like that of Laura's between good and bad cosmetics or dresses (46). He is adroit, as she is, in a world of social appearances and knows no other. Doubtless they make love but, on the one occasion where we see them alone together, their conversation is not about each other:

> The Count and Laura found their boat at last,
> And homeward floated o'er the silent tide,
> Discussing all the dances gone and past;

> The dancers and their dresses, too, beside:
> Some little scandals eke; . . .
>
> (87)

Elsewhere the Count supplies Laura, as needed, with lemonade (65) or is 'at her elbow with her shawl' (85). The perspective here is satirical rather than endorsing. However, it is useful to compare Byron's presentation of the Count with the poem 'A Letter from Artemisia in the Town to Chloe in the Country' by John Wilmot, Earl of Rochester, in which a husband dismissed by his wife is viciously described thus:

> The necessary thing bows and is gone

We see that Laura's Count, though almost as servile, is not satirized so straightforwardly. Byron explains that

> I fear I have a little turn for satire,
> And yet methinks the older that one grows
> Inclines us more to laugh than scold, though laughter
> Leaves us so doubly serious shortly after
>
> (79)

Beppo's return, in particular, fixes a comic rather than satiric presumption. The return itself is handled superbly. At the ball, Beppo appears in a Turkish costume that belongs both to the adventurous male world from which he has come and to the playful, feminine world of deceptive appearance to which he has returned. He stares at his wife, who no longer recognizes him. The stare appears to threaten Laura's confidence, for it proceeds not from her customary world of social flirtation but from a forgotten past and from an independent male spirit. Next, Laura and her Count return by boat in the early hours to their palace, talking of trivia, as we have seen. Cleverly chosen phrases suggest here the alien freshness and silence of the morning, as the gondola glides homewards with its chattering inmates. There, suddenly (Byron deftly retrieves the ancient poetic 'lo' in order to mask the shock), the returned and unrecognized husband confronts them (87). Momentarily, as Beppo reveals his identity and claims his wife, we anticipate a tragic finale. This is because Laura and the Count are no longer supported by their customary social setting but have been briefly placed before the elemental, the 'silent tide', as they would be in one of Byron's Oriental tales. Beppo himself is a wronged, pirate figure loyal to memories of the past, just like any of Byron's heroes. He is instantly assailed, however, as they never are, by the ordinary accommodations of day-to-day life. The Count produces his assured social skills:

> But the Count courteously invited in
> The stranger, much appeased by what he heard:
>   'Such things, perhaps, we'd best discuss within,'
> Said he; 'don't let us make ourselves absurd
>   In public, by a scene, nor raise a din,
>
> (90)

Once inside Laura dominates everything by her vital response to all present appearances:

> Now Laura, much recover'd, or less loth
> To speak, cries 'Beppo! What's your pagan name?
> Bless me! your beard is of amazing growth!
>
> (91)

By so doing, she instantly establishes supremacy over him:

> 'Beppo! that beard of yours becomes you not;
>   It shall be shaved before you're a day older:
> Why do you wear it? Oh! I had forgot —
>   Pray don't you think the weather here is colder?
> How do I look? You shan't stir from this spot
>   In that queer dress . . .
>
> (93)

Beppo is subdued, as well he might be, by his wife's ridiculous but rightly irresistible vitality of present perception, which dissolves any male fixity of purpose, memory or revengeful intentions. Laura's garrulity imposes on Beppo's silence. Byronic heroes don't say very much. Laura tames hers by this torrent of words. Instead he settles down to tell the tale of his Oriental adventures for the amusement of Venetian dinner-parties (98).

The narrator's poise and Beppo's adventures indicate a male independence that makes the Count's life-style seem ignominious; but all three are willingly held by the supreme vitality of Laura herself, who represents Woman as such, though not all women are like her.

Women are not diversified in *Beppo* as the narrator, Beppo and the Count are. The Count himself, however, is not really distinguishable from a host of other possible male escorts. He has, as they have, a range of social accomplishments, leisure and sufficient youth to render him decorous and serviceable. Greater definition than this could be gained only by a man declaring his independence of this world, where his passion is taken for granted, and becoming a wanderer like Beppo. Similarly, memory does not diversify women or their courtiers in Venice, for they live exclusively in the present. They are, as it were, in league with each present moment, and their art and nature render that attractive and sufficient. Venice lives like this.

Of course this must be a selective view. Byron's poetry knows other Venices than this. The old, for instance, can no longer be caught up in this sufficient present (see stanza 55) and Byron gives a telling account of the inability of ladies and pleasure to survive the cold inspection of morning light and 'after dancing dare the dawn' (83). Even Laura,

> ... knew it would not do at all
> To meet the daylight after seven hours' sitting
> Among three thousand people at a ball,
>
> (85)

Beppo's return is reinforced by this sense of the awkwardly clear light in which he challenges Laura and the Count. However, they successfully impose their bright surface chatter and habitual poise on this threatening presence. Both the narrator and Venice itself are, as it were, too much in league with Laura for her to be dethroned. For though she is, like Venice, artificial in manner, self-regarding and superficial in concern, Laura is a force of Nature that cannot be resisted. Like Venice too she is 'blooming still'. Her charms are increased by age.

In the early tales men refuse to yield their separate spheres of interest but cannot live without woman's tenderness. For both these reasons they are doomed. In *Beppo* the sexes naturally fuse their interests, though in fact this means that women rule. Although a price is paid, it appears to be worthwhile. It is perhaps ironical and instructive that *Beppo* seems to be addressed in the first instance to male readers, whereas the early tales were immensely popular with women, including, surprisingly, Jane Austen. But this mention of the poem's readers reminds us that *Beppo*, though written from and about Italy, is written to an English audience. The poem makes great play with this.

BEPPO: ENGLAND AND ITALY

Beppo is subtitled 'A Venetian Story'. It is a story about Venice and about Venetian ways. Just as Byron's Oriental tales depend upon exotic locations and behaviour, so Venice authorizes Byron's story and poem.

It is, however, systematically contrasted with England and English ways. The narrator, familiar with both life-styles, plays one off against the other. At times the poem sounds like a letter written from Italy to England:

> It was the Carnival, as I have said
>   Some six and thirty stanzas back, and so
> Laura the usual preparations made,
>   Which you do when your mind's made up to go
> To-night to Mrs Boehm's masquerade,
>   Spectator, or partaker in the show;
> The only difference known between the cases
> Is – *here*, we have six weeks of 'varnish'd faces.'
>
> (56)

In lines like these Byron seems to be addressing his contemporary English audience directly. 'You may be going to Mrs Boehm's masquerade [the details of this Byron had read in the *Morning Chronicle* for 27 June 1817], but what goes on for one evening in England is "here", that is in Venice, an affair of six weeks.' The tone is less enthusiastic about Italy than usual.

Normally Italy is celebrated and England is put down in *Beppo*. Gondoliers have similar problems to English coachmen (86) but are more exotic (19–20). Vineyards form the painted backdrop of English theatres but in Italy they are 'from tree to tree/Festoon'd' (41), for Italy is a living theatre that does not separate the wished intensities of art from day-to-day experience. Byron provides too a brilliant vignette of the gaucherie of a young English girl's 'coming out':

> 'Tis true, your budding Miss is very charming,
>   But shy and awkward at first coming out,
> So much alarm'd, that she is quite alarming,
>   All Giggle, Blush; half Pertness, and half Pout;
> And glancing at *Mamma*, for fear there's harm in
>   What you, she, it, or they, may be about,
> The nursery still lisps out in all they utter –
> Besides, they always smell of bread and butter.
>
> (39)

There is an affectionate cruelty in this which implies a whole world of sexual embarrassment as normal in English life. The contrast with the relaxed and sophisticated Venetian women is wholly to their advantage, just as later in the poem we admire their superior robustness:

> But where an English woman sometimes faints,
>   Italian females don't do so outright;
> They only call a little on their saints,
>   And then come to themselves, almost or quite;
>
> (89)

The poem depends upon this simple reiterated contrast between Italian sunshine and accommodation of sexuality with English 'cloudy climate, and our chilly women' (49). English day-to-day doings are typified in the newspaper entry 'trifling bankruptcies in the Gazette' (49). However, things are never as simple as this in Byron. He simplifies and exaggerates Venetian life doubtless, but he is at pains to suggest a whole set of idioms, manners and prevailing notions in Italian ways and juxtapose them with English habits. None of Byron's great contemporaries, except Walter Scott, could suggest so deftly as he the whole workings and character of a society. In *Beppo* we encounter two whole societies in miniature. England comes off worse, though it has its compensations. Byron himself is inside and outside English experience. For instance, when he describes the Venetian Ridotto ('a hall/Where people dance, and sup, and dance again'), he says that it is like 'our Vauxhall' but the Ridotto 'can't be spoilt by rain' (58). Then he comments on the people who go there:

> The company is mix'd (the phrase I quote is
> As much as saying they're below your notice);

This way of talking 'is the case in England' (60). Byron is here making fun of English class snobbery while at the same time deliciously using its registers in a peculiarly English, ironical way that is superior to some (but not all) kinds of English snobbery yet still implies the vulgarity of Italian high society. The manipulation of tone is superb and thoroughly English, not Italian. Similarly, in the three splendid stanzas (47–9) in which he praises England, we notice at once the evident ironies of

> I like the Habeas Corpus (when we've got it);
>
> (47)
>
> Our little riots just to show we are free men,
>
> (49)

and the disdainful reference to the Battle of Waterloo in

> And greatly venerate our recent glories,
> And wish they were not owing to the Tories.
>
> (49)

But there is another strain too. Byron's nostalgia for 'a sea-coal fire', 'a beef-steak' and 'a pot of beer' is not faked. British government is imperfect and not without tyrannical leanings, but there is freedom 'of the press and quill'. Though 'parliamentary debates' may be dull, they are superior to the complete lack of political life and the thorough-going censorship of Venice. Even 'our recent glories' contrast all too evidently with the just as recent extinction of Venetian independence. Byron says that

> ... at the moment when I fix my story,
> The sea-born city was in all her glory.
>
> (10)

Like *Don Juan*, then, *Beppo* is set some way in the past but both make constant allusion to the present. The present condition of Venice in 1817 (ruled by Austria) was anything but 'glory'. There is something about male-dominated, English efficiency (and its rather sexless but clubbable self-satisfactions) that is not without an attraction of its own. In England things work too, though different things and different priorities. The scatter of English proper names in the poem (Monmouth Street, the Strand, Harvey's Sauce, Dandies, Shakespeare, Wilberforce, Walker's Lexicon) is not there simply for their discrediting in comparison with colourful Italian names. Reading the poem we experience two very different styles of life, both of which have drawbacks and both of which can be loved. Though the poem principally celebrates Venice, we can see England and Venice as making a success of what the other cannot encompass. So, in the very act of simplifying our choice for us, Byron does not let us forget that it is a simplification. He has a genius for this.

The principal feature of Venetian life that distinguishes it from England, provides the substance of the commentary and brings about the dénouement is the southern European institution of the *cavaliere servente*. In this arrangement a married lady is allowed, indeed almost expected, to have one or more lovers and not to be faithful to her husband; however, certain conventions must still be observed. The male lovers must not be unfaithful (though they may be married), and family and social obligations must be respected. The arrangement is practical in that human preferences for illicit pleasures and the need for social stability are both satisfied. At the same time it allows men and women to feel that they are living romantically and to sustain a heightened love-language that comes, ultimately, from medieval Courtly Love. In these ways it compared favourably with Regency England where, it is implied, men and women were left with insufficient sexual nourishment and poetic leaven in their daily diet. Byron enjoys retailing this scandalous arrangement back to his English audience who expect tales of high passion from him and, though claiming a superior morality, make a mess of their emotional lives, divorce frequently and thrive on hypocrisy.

As we have seen, there is nevertheless something ridiculous in these pre-packed arrangements for Latin lovers, and the Count is not presented as remarkable for his sexual or poetic licences. The gaiety of festive Venice itself and the narrator's qualified but real enthusiasm for Laura and what she represents more or less carry us over these difficulties.

It must be said that although the poem celebrates women, it scarcely does so from what we would now call a feminist standpoint. Intellectual women get short shrift in *Beppo* and 'literary lady' (76) is a term of abuse. But we would be wrong to deduce that women are treated simply as sex objects. Neither men nor women can exist apart from their sexuality in the poem. Men are tethered by this, if anything, rather more than women. We are indeed given a glimpse of a third society, neither Venetian nor English, which does treat women as sex objects and that is Turkish:

> 'Tis said they use no better than a dog any
>   Poor woman, whom they purchase like a pad;
> They have a number, though they ne'er exhibit 'em,
> Four wives by law, and concubines 'ad libitum.'
>
> (70)

Turkish women pass their lives 'in doing nothing,/Or bathing, nursing, making love, and clothing' (71). This society is contrasted with that of England, where women are allowed to be interested in 'chemistry', 'mathematics', 'Religious novels, moral tales' (78) but seem to achieve neither final intellectual distinction nor sexual grace. Within the poem, therefore, however much it may annoy present opinion, treating women as sex objects and treating them as men in disguise are seen as comparable distortions. There is something deeply touching about Beppo's long look, neither English nor Turkish, at his lovely wife who does not recognize him:

> Our Laura's Turk still kept his eyes upon her,
>   Less in the Mussulman than Christian way,

Which seems to say, 'Madam, I do you honour,
  And while I please to stare, you'll please to stay.'
Could staring win a woman, this had won her,
  But Laura could not thus be led astray:
She had stood fire too long and well, to boggle
Even at this stranger's most outlandish ogle.

(81)

This is Byron's most sure-footed comedy. It is ironical that Laura refuses to be 'led astray' by Beppo's look for she is, in this, disloyal to her unrecognized husband; but we register too the tenderness and force of Beppo's look, which is sexual though not lustful, flirtatious or peremptory. There is an underlying sadness in the inappropriateness of Laura's self-confidence here, so well used as she is to provoke, expect and ignore the indiscriminate stare of strangers. All these reservations are swept away of course, when Beppo himself submits to Laura and Venetian ways in the last stanzas of the poem, for our laughter too in this English poem is firmly on Venice's side.

BEPPO: SERIOUS LAUGHTER

It may be thought that we have spent too long on the story of *Beppo* itself. Narrative, it is true, takes up fewer stanzas than digression. We are at least as much struck by the narrator's personality and the Venetian panorama that he unfolds as by the brief story of Laura, the Count and Beppo. The story, however, epitomizes Venetian vitality and its casual transformation of wayward human passions into workable social patterns. For the most part the digressions are not digressive, despite the narrator's mock apology for them, but an elaborate and detailed confirmation of the narrative viewpoint. The story is vital to our acceptance of the whole poem.

Beppo is a deliberately slight poem. Like the Venetian Carnival it is a whole world for a while, although it cannot be one for ever. It is not a shallow or cynical poem, however, for what it celebrates is worth celebrating and the poem implies some subtle reservations about its recommended values. We have mentioned some of these in passing, but can pursue here a little further the seriousness of Byron's laughter.

The narrator, for example, is relaxed, fluent and responds with infectious exuberance to Venice and its Lauras; however, we catch him occasionally when he is out of sorts:

> They went to the Ridotto ('tis a place
>   To which I mean myself to go to-morrow,
> Just to divert my thoughts a little space,
>   Because I'm rather hippish, and may borrow
> Some spirits, guessing at what kind of face
>   May lurk beneath each mask; and as my sorrow
> Slackens its pace sometimes, I'll make, or find
> Something shall leave it half an hour behind).
>
> (64)

Here, momentarily, the fun apparatus of Venice seems designed to hide and draw attention away from a radical pointlessness in the narrator's existence and in the Venetian faces 'beneath each mask'. There is a similar wry acknowledgement in stanza 62. Then too, as is always the case with Byron, the religious vocabulary of the poem carries more weight than immediately appears.

Beppo opens with an account of the Carnival that takes place in 'All countries of the Catholic persuasion'. The Venetian Carnival frames the action of the poem. Carnival-type festivals, in fact, go back a very long way and are closely bound up with the religious origins of comedy. A Catholic carnival is a time of festivity and licence but it is, literally, a 'farewell to flesh' (6) and a precursor of Lenten fasting and penitence for sin. Carnival authorizes topsy-turvy behaviour of all kinds, though it forbids attacks on religion (3–4). From a nineteenth-century, English, Protestant perspective, both the licence and the restrictions here are alien and ridiculous. The narrator, who is partly a detached English outsider in Venice, makes rather superior fun of both. However, when the narrator, in his other guise as participant, praises the world of Carnival, the accompanying religious perspective cannot be shaken off. The number of references to 'sin' in the poem is surprising. Most of these are ironical, though 'sad centuries of sin and slaughter' (80) is not. Nevertheless 'sin', however used, is the preferred word even in the most casual of contexts:

> In such affairs there probably are few
> Who have not had this pouting sort of squabble,
> From sinners of high station to the rabble.
>
> (53)

The snobbish use of the word 'rabble', for instance, is delicately undercut by the phrase 'sinners of high station', which reminds us that human rank and values are not the same as God's judgement. The narrator mocks the very tone of voice that he is using. In the next stanza it is even harder to disentangle the intended resonance:

> But, on the whole, they were a happy pair,
>   As happy as unlawful love could make them;
> The gentleman was fond, the lady fair,
>   Their chains so slight, 'twas not worth while to break them;
> The world beheld them with an indulgent air;
>   The pious only wish'd 'the devil take them!'
> He took them not; he very often waits,
> And leaves old sinners to be young ones' baits.
>
> (54)

Here the poet makes fun of 'The pious' who demand God's instant back-up for their moral condemnations, but his ironic diagnosis of the devil's strategy in leaving the old to corrupt the young is, though amusing, trenchantly orthodox and to the point.

In this way (and there are many more examples) the poem keeps alive in us what the Carnival temporarily puts aside. Human pleasures are good in themselves but they are disorderly and destructive too. Although the rival intensity of religion is mocked in the poem, we are not allowed to forget its discernments or rigours; at times we make evaluations that presuppose its truth. It seems too, particularly from an English perspective, that there is some necessary link between Italian love of life and Italian acceptance of religious boundaries and signs. The poem in this way offers a double perspective on the pleasures that it so casually handles.

We may add at this point those reminders of 'languishing with years' (55) that challenge the gaiety 'on restless tiptoe' (2) that Venice alone tolerates. Most poignant of all is Laura's recognition of passing time when she understands that it is Beppo whom, six years later, she now sees:

> '. . . How short your hair is! Lord! how grey it's grown!'
>
> (93)

In these ways *Beppo* is less one-sided than it may seem, but it is not *Don Juan*. *Don Juan*, as we shall see, allows equal force to negative and positive energies and is ruthless in both. *Beppo* enlists our support for a comic point of view and reminds us of what this leaves out, but it does not set out to trouble us with the discrepancies between the two. It is intended to be intelligent fun and, as such, to challenge contemporary sense of what a good poem was supposed to be. Contemporary taste was on the look-out for 'That charming passage in the last new poem' (72) or for poetic intensity of some kind. *Beppo* also challenged, as *Don Juan* was to do more profoundly, the emerging, rather stuffy, moral consensus of nineteenth-century England. The confidence with which Byron did this is dazzling, though it is not crude.

Some critics have argued (or more usually, just assumed) that Beppo, Laura and the Count end up in a *ménage à trois* – or, at any rate, that the Count and Laura keep up their old relationship. That suggestion is not ruled out by the poem, for Beppo and the Count 'were always friends' but Laura 'sometimes put him in a rage' (99). The ending is left open. Conrad in *The Corsair* ends up with two women; Laura in *Beppo* ends up with two men. But to insist on this as an arrangement would be absurd and leave the poem with a final knowing leer. While Byron may have disliked nineteenth-century primness, he would not be enamoured of our rationalized permissiveness. Byron's conclusion is as generous as his poem and as his nature. The strong forces of Beppo and Laura are reunited without a dramatic clash but, inevitably, with some hint of future tensions. However, Beppo's old age makes him 'some amends' for his early sufferings and the Count, who could be despised or dismissed, continues too beyond the end of the poem in a world of toleration and forgiveness that owes more to Byron's delicate sense of comedy than to any Venetian strategies of co-habitation.

Beppo is not Byron's greatest poem but it is pleasing and, arguably, the most successful of Byron's tales. It can be compared, for instance, with W. H. Auden's poem 'Letter to Lord Byron' (in *Letters from Iceland*), which is a deliberate and clever echo of Byron's manner and plays off Iceland against England much as Byron uses Venice in *Beppo*. We may then catch some sense of how difficult it is to write like this. Both Auden and Byron deploy a large vocabulary and have a fine ear for placing the right word in the right place. *Beppo* remains the better poem. It does not have the remorseless intensity of *Parisina* or the large-scale confidence of *The Island* but, line by line, it is better written than either of them. On the other hand we will not take *Beppo* seriously enough if we do not take Byron's other tales seriously too.

The Vision of Judgement and Byron's Satires

(The first section gives a brief account of satire in general and Byron's other satires. The second section is entirely concerned with The Vision of Judgement.*)*

The Satires

What is satire? Many different things have, at different times, been called 'satires' and we should not look for too strict a definition. As always, if we really want to understand something, we have to go into its history. We can do this here only in the briefest outline.

The distant origins of satire seem to be in invective, curses and hostile charm-sayings directed, for example, against enemies immediately before battle. The earliest forms of prophecy arose, perhaps, in similar circumstances. These distant origins impart a permanent character of vituperative energy to satire and declare its public field. They may explain too why satire may originate in private feuds but it always has to convince us that there is some public good in, and public audience for, the ritual discrediting that it undertakes. Not all Byron's satires sufficiently satisfy these criteria.

Satire has a long history and we should identify at least one other strand in it that offsets the coarse energies that founded it. The Latin poet Juvenal (A.D. 60–130) is a good example of these coarse energies but his predecessor Horace (65–8 B.C.) makes of satire something quite different. Horace's satires are based on conversational manner. They are urbane verse-letters addressed to friends and patrons. Horace has definite moral views but he is detached, tolerant and witty. Here we are less aware of overriding public good and more of necessary social adjustments, good sense and extreme sophistication. An important part of the subject-matter too becomes the distinction between good and bad poetry.

In English poetry we find both these models operating in the greatest period of English satire from about 1670–1750. Pope translated and imitated Horace; Dryden translated Juvenal. Together they elevated satire to an entirely new role and importance in English culture. Dryden and Pope were brilliantly successful, though their success had two unfortunate consequences. Neither poet should be thought of simply as a satirist, but this is what happened. Dryden's visionary concern for history and Pope's wonderful tenderness were ignored. Secondly, their success was such that it was neither possible to do what they did better nor, on the other hand, was it easy to escape their influence and do something else.

By and large, Romantic poetry established itself by finally breaking the decisive hold of satire, and Pope and Dryden, on the course of English poetry, but this is by no means as straightforward a business as is often suggested.

Byron loved Pope and Dryden. He defended Pope in particular with extraordinary passion. There was indeed something of a revival of interest in Pope and Dryden in the early nineteenth century. George Crabbe (1754–1832) was called by Byron 'the postscript of the Augustans'. Even Keats tried hard to learn something from Dryden when he was writing 'Lamia'. Other Romantic poets, Shelley and Blake for example, often thought of as visionary lyricists, wrote a surprising amount of satirical verse. So did Robert Burns.

There were other difficulties, however, besides the problem of not imitating Pope and Dryden's style. The audience for poetry had shifted since the 1700s. Then it had been worthwhile and innovatory to struggle for a sound, well-balanced style that could outdo even French in lucidity and poise, and reflected the alliance between aristocratic style and bourgeois good sense in European culture. That alliance was symbolically disrupted by the French Revolution. Now middle-class taste everywhere insisted upon excitement, oddity and strong feeling. These made up a good recipe for Gothic horror stories or for Byron's Oriental tales but not for a satirical defence of the public good. Satire now worked best if clearly linked with the prophetic strain when, as so often in Blake and Shelley, its true character was more or less disguised as something else.

Byron, the most consistent satirist of the period and by far the best, helps us to thread our way through these intricacies. In one poem, *The Vision of Judgement* (1822), he achieves the impossible. He writes a satire wholly fresh in manner yet clearly performing identical functions in all major respects to those of the great public satires of Pope and Dryden that he so much admired.

We risk distortion at the very outset, however. Just as Pope and Dryden are, even now, still sometimes classified as 'Augustan satirists' as though that were the end of the matter, so Byron, with even less reason, is sometimes hailed as a satirist as though he therefore stopped being a Romantic poet. All too easily the word 'satire', even when used as praise, becomes an excuse for cutting a poem or poet down to size, usually small to extra-small. It is as though our own good sense is merely confirmed by the poem. In the case of Pope and Dryden, what is crucial is not so much their satire of heroic poetry or of their own unheroic age in the light of heroic standards, but simply the thoroughfare that they established between satire and heroic perspectives. So with Byron, it is not as though he is neatly undoing Romanticism with his satire (though sometimes he does just this), but that he is opening up and establishing links between Romantic and satiric dispositions. We can see this as part of a wider European pattern sometimes called 'Romantic irony', but Byron's contribution is quite distinctive. This is what is exciting about him and we should not try to tidy it all up too much. A similarly puzzling mixture of vision, irony and satire can be found in T. S. Eliot's *The Waste Land* (1922).

It is not all a success story. Byron wrote seven major poems that are indisputably satires. These are *English Bards and Scotch Reviewers* (1809), *Hints from Horace* (written 1811), *The Curse of Minerva* (written 1811), *The Waltz* (1813), *The Vision of Judgement* (1822), *The Blues* (1823) and *The Age of Bronze* (1823). Of these only *The Vision of Judgement* is an unqualified success. Four of them, *Hints from Horace*, *The Curse of Minerva*, *The Waltz* and *The Blues*, are complete flops. Byron's poems are often flawed but nearly all of them are readable and, in some sense, work. Hazlitt said that Byron was 'never dull or tedious'. It is odd, then, that four of his satires should be unread and unreadable. Certainly if Byron's genius were thought to lie simply in satire these would be unpalatable facts. The reason for the failure of *The Waltz* or *The Blues*, for instance, which lightly satirize the new dance form and literary conventions, is that their indignation is not related to wider energies or concerns. Byron may dislike both, but there is insufficient consensus in his society to support his antipathy and he does not tap deeper reservoirs of feeling in himself. Although *English Bards* and *The Age of Bronze* are much more successful, the first does not completely convince us that Byron's views on the current state of literature transcend his own private likes and dislikes, and the second, a satire on the contemporary political scene with an impressive European perspective, is presented from a partisan viewpoint. It is as though Byron does not quite expect us to share his indignation. While there may be energy, even genius, in these poems, they do not carry that strange exhilaration to be found in Pope's *The Dunciad* or Dryden's *Absalom and Achitophel*, which, bearing us along with it, effortlessly engages our agreement. We will find exactly this exhilaration in *The Vision of Judgement*, however. We find it too, needless to say, throughout *Don Juan*, which, though satirical, is not in my view a satire.

The Vision of Judgement

ORIGINS AND THE QUARREL WITH SOUTHEY

Satire nearly always originates in some particular circumstances or abuse, but it has to convince us that its ridicule of this abuse serves some general purpose and vindicates some precious feature of communal life. We must begin, then, with the particular circumstances that *The Vision of Judgement* rises out of and immortalizes, though our purpose must not be to linger there or think that the poem is confined to these circumstances.

The Vision of Judgement describes the arrival of the recently dead George III at the gates of heaven, the resultant dispute as to whether he belongs inside or to hell, and comes to a farcical conclusion as the King slips into heaven under cover of a celestial riot provoked by the reading of a very boring poem.

Obviously George III's death is one particular circumstance upon which the poem depends. The other is a poem about this event by the Poet Laureate Robert Southey, called *A Vision of Judgement*. This is the boring poem that drives the inhabitants of Byron's vision mad. Byron's preface to the poem makes it clear that he is more concerned with ridiculing Southey's poem than with attacking the King. Byron's *Vision* is designed to outlaugh and outlast Southey's. We catch here something of the spirit of that ancient confrontation between rival bards before a battle or at a funeral, panegyrizing or mocking rival chieftains. Southey's poem is unread (it is hard nowadays to find an edition in which to read it), whereas Byron's poem still exists in popular editions. So Byron won. How did the battle begin?

A quarrel had been brewing for some time between the two poets. Byron had already attacked Southey in his dedication to *Don Juan*. This dedication, at Byron's direction, remained unpublished, but its existence and nature were known to Southey and others. When Southey published his *Vision of Judgement* (11 April 1821), his preface went out of its way to attack Byron, whom he accused of setting up a 'Satanic school' of poetry. The famous critic William Hazlitt (Byron later satirized him as 'Scamp' in *The Blues*) had popularized the notion that poets could be grouped into schools in his *Lectures on the English Poets* (1818–19). Byron hated such theorizing and the word 'Satanic' must have particularly stung him. Undoubtedly there are Satanic elements in Byron's character and fictions, as we have seen (pp. 12, 28–9, 34–5), but he is primarily a great moral poet in love with life for all its dark paradoxes, alert to human follies, and not without real religious reverence. His reply to Southey's charge is to draw a brilliant and sympathetic new portrait of Satan in his own poem, while balancing this with the energy and beauty of St Michael, Satan's 'former friend and future foe'. Although Byron uses Satan to underline George's faults, the poem does not endorse all of Satan's attitudes. At the end Satan too is treated as a figure of fun. There is a more generous morality and a more substantial reverence in Byron's poem than in Southey's pompous verses.

Southey was not a negligible foe. He was an accomplished poet of whom Byron had written in his journal in 1813, 'He has *passages* equal to anything.' But Byron had two principled objections to him apart from the personal quarrel between them. Southey was now a Tory and, as Poet Laureate, in some sense represented the Government. However, Southey had begun as a radical who sympathized with revolutionary movements. Byron saw him, therefore, as a turncoat who supported what Byron regarded as reactionary policies at home and abroad.

Byron's own political views were complex. He sympathized with political change and hated tyrannical practices, but he was suspicious of revolutionary cant and respected the continuities of history. He could like and admire Tories such as George Canning, the Foreign Secretary, William Gifford the critic, and his 'good comrade' Sir Walter Scott the novelist. Scott had, in fact, rejected the offer of Laureateship that Southey had accepted. It was Southey's earnestness and arrogance, his apparent indifference to his former loyalties, that outraged Byron, who remained steady in his own friendships and instincts. Southey's *Vision* consigned all the big anti-Tory voices of the recent past to hell. Byron was careful to allow George III, whom he did not like, into heaven.

In poetic matters, on the other hand, Southey was far from conservative. He boasts in his preface that his verses 'have none of the customary characteristics of English versification'. Byron detested such claims, for, in matters of verse, he was deeply conservative. He disliked the attacks on Pope's manner that were part of the increasingly polarized

57

debate about that poet. Southey, turncoat and reactionary in politics, innovator in poetry, was therefore the antithesis of Byron and, as Poet Laureate, publicly represented the old ways in government and the new ways in verse. Byron, in fact, found it hard to get his poem published because of its subject-matter. When it did appear in a new journal called the *Liberal*, the publisher was, eventually, fined.

Byron's literary conservatism needs some explaining. Though words like 'original', 'innovatory' and 'challenging' become staler each day we use them, we still find ourselves expecting all great art to epitomize these qualities. This is because Southey's theories (and those of Romantic poets in general) won the critical battle in the early nineteenth century, since they better fitted the use that the middle classes were to make of art. It was quite permissible to reproduce selected Gothic effects in architecture or ballads in order to heighten dreamlike intensities. Writers wrote about the Middle Ages, for instance, as they might about some far-off exotic country. Byron believed, on the contrary, that using the past was more a matter of letting the past use him and that this was how all great poetry was written. Byron's reasoning, though more instinctive in character, resembles that of T. S. Eliot in his famous essay 'Tradition and the Individual Talent'. Byron's *The Vision of Judgement* must therefore be at once an example of a truer morality than Southey's and it must demonstrate that writing with some 'of the customary characteristics of English versification' does not preclude freshness and energy. In both these aims it succeeds.

We will need to delve further into Byron's use of tradition in order to demonstrate this. If Byron is right about tradition, the discoveries we make should resemble those in genetics, for thoughts, feelings, styles and words have coherent, if sometimes confusing, histories that cannot be jettisoned or selected according to individual whim. A poem works best when its complex ancestry is allowed, and seen, to act through it. We might be confused, for instance, to discover that Southey too claims precedents for his poetry. His un-English versification is based on Greek metres and he invites us at the beginning of his *Vision* to compare his procedures with those of Dante in *The Divine Comedy*. Dante's great poem is also a vision of many judgements in a supernatural world. What is at stake in these rival ways of claiming continuity with the past? Should we look to museum catalogues rather than to genetics to provide an analogy? Let us examine the opening lines of both poems and see what they tell us. This is the opening of Southey's poem:

'Twas at the sober hour when the light of day is receding
And from surrounding things the hues wherewith day has adorn'd them
Fade, like the hopes of youth, till the beauty of earth is departed:
Pensive, though not in thought, I stood at the window, beholding
Mountain and lake and vale;

And this is the opening of Byron's:

> Saint Peter sat by the celestial gate:
>   His keys were rusty, and the lock was dull,
> So little trouble had been given of late;
>   Not that the place by any means was full,

Byron begins his poem directly. We are already in the sky. Southey begins with himself, looking out over the Lake District where he lived. Byron is matter-of-fact about his odd location. Southey is elevated about his more usual one. Byron's tone, particularly in line 4, is close to conversation. Southey distances us from ordinary speech. Nevertheless Byron immediately imagines, however ironically, an unimaginable place (the gate of heaven) whereas Southey is only dressing up in verse an image of himself and what he sees out of his window in the evening. Dante's verse is not like either of these here, but it is closer to Byron's than to Southey's. Byron, like Dante, seems to see directly what he presents to us and details an unearthly perspective with a factual eye. Southey's most typical poems were, in fact, fantastic in character. He made things up. Byron's imagination, on the contrary, is a way of seeing things as they are but in an imagined perspective. When Southey comes to write *A Vision of Judgement*, therefore, we sense that it is made up as he goes along, while Byron's poem is immediately convincing. This turns the tables on Southey in unexpected ways. Byron is not only more matter-of-fact, he is also more of a visionary poet than Southey. For throughout nearly all of Byron's poem we do not imagine ourselves to be in the world as we know it but in some wholly other dimension, in space, a comic theatre, and before heaven. In this Byron deeply resembles Dante.

Dante, of course, is not primarily a humorist or satirist; but the European tradition of vision writing, in which he is supreme, is tangled up with dark humour. We would never suspect this from Southey, and Romantic poetry in general tends to conceal the connection. Byron's preface is signed QUEVEDO REDIVIVUS which makes the connection for us. Franciso Quevedo (1580–1645) was a Spanish writer who produced a famous group of *Suenos*, or 'Visions'. One of these was 'Of the Last Judgement'. Quevedo mixes up macabre humour, piety, ribaldry and reverence in bewildering ways. Long before Quevedo, the Roman poet Seneca (*d.* A.D. 65) wrote a humorous satire with a very long name, *Apocolocyntosis*, on the official deification of the Emperor Claudius after his death. This is an exact parallel to Byron's satire on George III's entry into heaven.

So classical, medieval and Renaissance traditions continue to live in Byron's poem, though they are not, as it were, picked up at a distance in the way nineteenth-century architects tried to reconstruct medieval effects. Byron gets back to the distant past via his immediate predecessors rather than by rejection of them. Pope and Dryden, heroes of Byron, had also satirized laureates and kings. Pope's great poem *The Dunciad* (1728, 1743) ridiculed Colley Cibber, then Poet Laureate, and, by implication, George II, his Queen and his ministers. Hence Southey's silly poem on George III presented Byron with an opportunity to match his predecessors on their own ground and show his contemporaries that the themes and purposes of Augustan verse could still hold good in George IV's England. But Byron wisely did not closely reproduce Pope and Dryden's style, as he had in *English Bards*. Instead he took *ottava rima*, the verse form already used for *Beppo* and the first five cantos of *Don Juan* (the rest were unwritten at that time), and adapted it for his new purposes.

Principally this meant virtually scrapping the narrator who is so crucial to the manner of *Beppo* and *Don Juan*. There are some thirty references to the narrator as 'I', but, apart from three stanzas on hell-fire (13–15), there is nothing like the continually interrupting narrator of *Don Juan* and *Beppo*. We remain, almost continuously, in neutral space. More than a third of the poem is taken up by dialogue between the angels, devils and spirits. The number of double rhymes is halved compared with the normal proportion in *Don Juan* and there is only one trisyllabic rhyme ('economy', 'one am I', 'alone am I', 53) and two smothered ones ('Castilian', 'civilian', 36; 'pinions', 'dominions, opinions', 103), whereas these play a major part in the comic effects of his other *ottava rima* poems. (For further general comments on the nature of Byron's *ottava rima*, see pp. 115–18.)

So Byron fashions his poem out of a carefully chastened version of his own most recent style, assumes something of the stance of Pope and Dryden towards his society and his subject-matter, and claims a different route (via Quevedo's odd *Suenos*) back to Dante and to classical poetry that convinces us of their inherent vitality far more than Southey's modern use of them. This is seen too in the use both poets make of their ultimate source for visions of judgement: the Bible. The irreverent Byron knew the Bible far better than Southey and is able to combine a whole series of allusions to Old and New Testaments for comic and serious purposes.

Byron's use of the Bible, more clearly than anything else, reveals his exact calculation of tone. Byron imagines what it is like to be everyone in his narrative; St Peter, for instance, exists vividly for us. He is cranky, impetuous and eager to resent a slight. He is furious that the recently arrived Louis XVI (guillotined in 1793) should claim to be a martyr just like the apostle. He is incensed too when Lucifer tells him that George III has always opposed Catholic Emancipation, for Peter is the first Pope. He resents St Paul because Paul was converted after Christ's death and is therefore a latecomer in comparison with the other apostles. From Peter's grumpy perspective, St Paul rather stole the show away from himself as chief apostle, so he refers to him as

> That fellow Paul – the parvenù!
> (20)

This character sketch is both deft and, though playfully inventive, bears a real resemblance to the traditional understanding of St Peter's character in the New Testament. As Byron observes, Peter has always 'been known/For an impetuous saint' (104). When we see him 'pattering' or 'pottering' with his keys (Byron's manuscript says 'potter'd' but editions vary), sweating with fear at Satan's arrival, or knocking Southey about with the same keys, we are laughing at a plausible human character within a humorous tradition not hostile to reverence of other kinds. We may usefully recall the similar treatment of biblical characters in medieval dramas, and Peter's sudden attack on Southey is modelled on his action in the New Testament when he cuts off the ear of the High Priest's servant. Byron is careful, however, to exclude God Himself from this banter. He is kept out of the poem altogether.

Byron's magnificent treatment of the confrontation between Michael and Satan, perhaps the best thing in the poem, shows that he can imagine figures of transcendent power as well as human pathos in his vision. Southey's poem, in comparison, is inept beyond anyone's belief in its imaginings. No angel or saint is realized with any force. Instead there are Gothic references to hermits and nuns. God ('the Presence') does appear in, and therefore blasphemously within, the action, and George III is welcomed first by a recently assassinated prime minister, then by several dead monarchs, assorted celebrities and his own family. There is something deeply unchristian in Southey's *Vision*, for it implies that the exalted shall be exalted even higher, and there is a half-heartedness in its imagination that constantly leads to absurdities. Would we see this so clearly if Byron's poem had not revealed authoritatively just how far outside central traditions of belief and idiom Southey's *Vision* is?

STRUCTURE

Many satires are virtually structureless, for they are linked to the idea of a medley or to the flow of a conversation or letter. Horace's satires and Byron's *The Age of Bronze* are like this. Other satires, such as Pope's *Rape of the Lock* or Orwell's *Animal Farm*, are structured by a narrative. Byron's *Vision* resembles these.

The structure Byron adopts is deceptively simple. The apparatus of a Judgement is set up and two judgements are given. Southey is knocked down and George III slips into heaven. Both these events and the summoning of witnesses for the Judgement are versions of Southey's episodes, but they are treated farcically. Byron himself seems to stand apart from the action. Once the scene is set before the gate of heaven, characters arrive in succession and talk just as they do in Dante's great poem. The sequence is, first George himself (who is not yet an inmate and scarcely says anything), then Satan, Michael, Wilkes, 'Junius' and finally Southey. Each of these is diverting, both in his present unearthly and past historical existence. All are fascinated by one another and this is one of the most effective means by which Byron convinces us of the reality of his other world. For example, between Michael and Satan 'There pass'd a mutual glance of great politeness' (35) and Wilkes, who had died twenty-three years before the King, exclaims on seeing him,

> and that soul below
> Looks much like George the Third, but to my mind
> A good deal older – Bless me! is he blind?'
>
> (68)

That detail reveals the fidelity of Byron's imagination. Wilkes does not function simply as a prosecution witness but responds with tenderness and shock to his stricken opponent. It comes as no surprise that, though critical of the King, he votes him into heaven. This may be, as Satan tartly observes, because Wilkes, from being George's foe, 'turn'd to half a courtier' before he died (72), but it is also part of the strategy of the poem. George is perceived as a bad king, although he is a vulnerable, bewildered human being with some virtues as well. The attacks on him occur in the two opening sections of the poem, first in the narrator's voice and then in Satan's, but the tone of the poem shifts away from this severity. We become separately interested in the quirky vitality of Byron's peopled sky. When Satan's two witnesses, Wilkes and 'Junius' (an anonymous eighteenth-century letter-writer), withdraw their charges against George or refuse to repeat them, the way is cleared for the humorous acceptance of the King's quick dash into heaven. At the same time the focus shifts away from bad kings (George) to bad writers (Southey) and the satire modulates into farce. In this way Byron is able to present an alternative perspective to Southey's view of recent English history and castigate the late King, while retaining our interest through a succession of independent characters and, almost unnoticed, adjusting the idiom from telling criticism to good-humoured fun. Southey invites us to compare his own poem with Dante's. Such comparison would be ludicrous. But Byron's handling of angels, devils and historical characters in an unearthly but precise location can fully stand comparison with a major episode in *The Divine Comedy*. The management of tone in Byron's poem, however, owes more to Shakespeare's comedy than to Dante's.

VOICE AND VOCABULARY

The English language has a much larger working vocabulary than most. We have at our disposal, therefore, a range of words of many different types. We distinguish 'registers' of diction based on class, context, linguistic origin, and so on.

Byron loves setting words of different types against one another. The effect is often comic, sometimes absurd, thought-provoking or moving. In Byron's *Vision* it makes us continually aware of the odd mixture of angels, saints, devils, kings and politicians in 'neutral space'. St Michael, for instance, talks like an aristocratic ambassador:

> Michael began: 'What wouldst thou with this man,
>   Now dead, and brought before the Lord? What ill
> Hath he wrought since his mortal race began,
>   That thou canst claim him?
>   (38)

If we had to imagine archangels speaking, then this would be an appropriate diction. But of course such a diction summons up associations (nowadays, perhaps, something like the speeches in United Nations) that become ridiculous here. Kings should speak something like this, but George III actually spoke in a notoriously different way in short repeated questions and continues to do so in the sky:

> The monarch, mute till then, exclaim'd, 'What! what!
> *Pye* come again? No more – no more of that!'
>
> (92)

The poet himself can talk like either of these and more to wonderful effect. The sudden opening of heaven's gate and the first appearance of St Michael from heaven, for instance, is handled like this:

> As things were in this posture, the gate flew
>   Asunder, and the flashing of its hinges
> Flung over space an universal hue
>   Of many-coloured flame, until its tinges
> Reach'd even our speck of earth, and made a new
>   Aurora borealis spread its fringes
> O'er the North Pole; the same seen, when ice-bound,
> By Captain Parry's crew, in 'Melville's Sound.'
>
> And from the gate thrown open issued beaming
>   A beautiful and mighty Thing of Light,
>
> (27, 28)

Here elevated phrases such as 'Asunder', 'universal hue', 'Aurora borealis', and the choice of 'issued' rather than the simpler 'came', establish St Michael's status, and the marvellous phrase 'A beautiful and mighty Thing of Light' suggests an elemental, superhuman force. The diction matches the picture. Flashes of the gate hinge cause a huge explosion of coloured light across the sky. The idea could be Milton's.

Elevated diction such as this suggests dignity and transcendence but, persisted in, may lack energy and warmth. Here, however, the constantly run-on lines, or enjambment, and the careful positioning of the verbs 'flew/Asunder' and 'Flung over space' imply energetic motion. As the sentence extends on to the end of the stanza, it loses some of this momentum, though this too exactly matches the way the original event peters out into 'tinges' that reach 'even our speck of earth'. Even these 'tinges' cause the amazing phenomenon (to our earth-bound eyes) of the

Northern lights, or 'Aurora borealis'. This sense of the immense distance between our world and Michael's heaven, or rather that suggestion of intolerable forces of light pent up in heaven that momentarily flash in the opening of heaven's gate, is reinforced by the deliberately prosaic reference to 'Captain Parry's crew' in 'Melville's Sound'. The human proper names sound absurd here. Yet from our perspective they indicate exotic voyagers who have witnessed amazing cosmic spectacles. The effect of this sudden shift of viewpoint is at once ludicrous and awe-inspiring. We should not let the tone mislead us here. Although the poem remains comic, the visionary imagination at work in it is that of the greatest poets, of Dante and Milton. Of course the poem opened with an opposite sense of heaven's gate, as we recall:

> Saint Peter sat by the celestial gate:
> His keys were rusty, and the lock was dull,

In these lines Byron is burlesquing Southey's *Vision*. In the lines on Michael's dramatic entry through the same gate he is transcending a pretended vision by the thing itself.

A main reason for reading and needing poetry is that it can recall us to a proper sense of amazement at the world; this is one of the things that it does best. Byron had this sense of astonishment at things acutely and he writes directly out of it. Here the style authenticates this sense of astonishment while at the same time, in the reference to Captain Parry, reminding us of our common-sense ways of dealing with things we cannot grasp. The angels similarly at times convince as huge celestial forces (it is very difficult for anyone nowadays to take angels seriously; Southey makes a hopeless mess of it), sometimes as birds (26), sometimes as politicians (62) and sometimes as comic properties (86). The great and silent spaces of the sky are filled with dialogue in all registers: political rhetoric (45), Irish oaths (59) and the horrible special voices that poets sometimes use to read their own verse (90).

Byron's style depends upon the deployment of voice. There are some effects in his verse that it would be hard to imagine in his speech, but, unlike some poets, Byron never tries to suppress voice altogether or replace it by an exclusively poetic register. Byron's *Vision*, on the contrary, is made real to us not only by the steadiness of his visual imagination but by the acutely heard speech-patterns of a cluster of individuated presences that rise up from 'neutral space' every time we read the poem.

65

VIEWPOINT

Byron is always concerned to be intelligible and to illuminate and effect other things than poetry by his verse. Hence he must say or present recognizable viewpoints forcefully and try to recommend them to his readers. At the same time he is always conscious of paradoxes of all kinds and hidden connections between things that may appear quite separate. His poetry catches our moral will yet enlarges our sense of the oddity of things. His task therefore is to be both straightforward and subtle, just as the traditions of European satire in general utilize delicate wit and crude abuse. What is *The Vision of Judgement* straightforward about?

Southey's poem reviewed George I I I's reign as a success story. There was something in this. Britain in 1820, after Napoleon's final defeat, was vastly more powerful and important that it had been in 1760 when George I I I became king. Byron is concerned to tell the other side of the story. From his point of view the most significant events in the last sixty years had been part of the progress of Liberty, in America (Independence), in France (Revolution) and throughout the continent. In England popular figures like Wilkes had spoken up for the people's liberties and serious efforts had been made to repeal the laws that prevented English Catholics from taking equal part in national life. To all this George I I I had been opposed. English will, policy and power, victorious at Waterloo, had played a decisive part in the restoration to power of the old monarchies throughout Europe in 1815. In this sense England, which Southey presented as the saviour of Europe, was, Byron thought, its enslaver. Waterloo itself is seen by him as 'the crowning carnage' (5) from which even the recording angels turn away in disgust. Byron is careful to acknowledge George's virtues as an individual and to declare that, though he 'shielded tyrants', he was 'no tyrant' himself (8). But the attack is clear, forceful and unequivocal.

Byron's attack on Southey is equally straightforward. The poem's shift from politics to poetry is, in a way, from larger to lesser concerns. But, like Pope or Dryden, Byron takes very seriously the spread of 'cant' and the decline in public taste. It is characteristic of satire to assert that there is a deep connection between politics, morality and style. Southey's poem gets all three things wrong. Southey is talented but, high-handed about literary tradition as he was, can write in a ridiculously unnatural way. Southey claims to occupy the central cultural space and speak for the heart of the nation. From Byron's perspective Southey is, however, a

'Laker': eccentric, unstable in his allegiances and a charlatan in his solemnity. Southey writes as a declared Christian poet. Byron, outraged by Southey's simple identification of his own judgements with those of God, shows us just how unchristian Southey's poem is in its snobbish and confident damnations. Southey typifies, in Byron's eyes, a new kind of 'Romantic' poetry that assumes the role of visionary far too readily. This facile claim to be 'creative' affronts common sense and true art in much the same way as the dunces in Pope's *The Dunciad*. Byron shows us, in his anti-Vision, the resilience and full play of consciousness needed to produce a true vision. It is a witty stroke, therefore, when Byron allows the reading of Southey's false *Vision* to destroy his own so that 'the whole spiritual show' vanishes (102).

All this is accomplished with great directness but not without playfulness too. Byron is at ease as Southey is not. Supremely confident, he can nevertheless present himself modestly. In his preface he presents his poem as 'not intended to be serious'. He can temper his trenchancy with generosity and delicacy. George himself, the subject of bitter comment, is sometimes treated with something like tenderness as he sits old, muffled in his shroud, surrounded by strange spirits (23). Even Southey, well and truly savaged, is allowed to be 'not an ill-favour'd knave' (94). Above all, the vast spaces and strange forces that Byron's poem realizes for us and in which he places his human beings, still locked in their strange fashions of speech and clothing (66–7), remind us how odd it is to preserve human judgements of good and evil, even Byron's, in the face of a universe whose energies, blankness and secret sources are beyond our comprehension. We shape the cosmos too readily in our own image and likeness. The poem, therefore, simultaneously gives clear judgements on characters and history, while at the same time holding all human judgements in abeyance and recommending charity.

We may summarize our findings like this. *Beppo* is a comic tale. *The Vision of Judgement* is a comic vision but it originates in response to Southey's version of George III's history, and it is this origin in a particular distortion which needs correcting that makes it a satire. The distortion, though particular, affects public affairs and issues; hence the conflict between Southey and Byron is for occupancy of that central space in a culture that the satirist and the prophet alike dispute. Though the poem includes conversations, it is not written in and out of conversation as *Beppo* and much of *Don Juan* are. The poet does not chat to the reader except in brief asides (e.g. 70–71), for the poem begins directly 'St Peter sat' and is not enclosed in a world of talk. It is not written by a talker but by a 'seer'. It is held together, ironically or not, by the old formulas of vision poetry: 'Lo! there came' (16), 'Michael flew forth' (30), 'The shadow came' (85).

Byron sets against this tableau the well-adjusted sound of myriad human voices ending in a babble, though separately maintained till then. The sophistication is evident but so too is the fun. We mark the lightness of touch as well as its exactness. Quite unlike any poem by Pope or Dryden, it rejoices to belong to their lineage. It also makes us reconsider our glib tendencies to draw lines of outright separation between Augustan and Romantic poetry or between 'satire' and 'vision'.

2. Don Juan

Sources, Influences and Themes

Don Juan is a massive poem although it remained unfinished at Byron's death. It is, for instance, more than twice as long as Wordsworth's *The Prelude*. Great poems, when they operate on this scale, recycle the methods and materials of earlier literature, while transforming them into a new and unpredictable life. Byron's poem has a recognizable style and manifest concerns, but it is far more inclusive and open to the unexpected than most of the long poems that preceded it. One of the surprises of the poem, and part of its greatness, is the way in which many different literary procedures and structures are brought and held together in it. We need to recognize at least some of these, so the major ones will will be indicated in this section.

One of the most striking features of *Don Juan* is its double focus. We are interested both in the adventures of Don Juan himself and in the character and digressions of the narrator. This effect is original and disconcerting, though Byron did have some precedents for it. Homer's *Odyssey*, for example, is an adventure poem dealing with the wanderings of Ulysses after the Trojan War, just as Byron is concerned with the wanderings of Juan. Homer's account of Ulysses's journey is constantly interrupted by a description of the world of the gods and their commentary upon, or interventions in, the world of mortals. This epic technique is surprisingly close to that of Byron's poem, which he half seriously calls 'epic' on a number of occasions. For, although the narrator is not a god, he is presented as simply an observing mind no longer active in the world himself. He does intervene in and control the world of Juan too, much like one of Homer's gods, because he is presented as writing the poem and manipulating its incidents. Such an Homeric technique had been used and parodied by the eighteenth-century novelist Henry Fielding in *Tom Jones*, which may have influenced Byron. Novels, histories and other works in prose certainly made an impression on him and, in this way, profoundly affected a long poem for the first time in English literature.

Although the adventures of Juan owe a great deal to the *Odyssey*, to *Tom Jones* and to Spanish and French picaresque novels of the seven-

69

teenth and eighteenth centuries, Byron's hero comes from a seventeenth-century Spanish play *El Burlador de Sevilla* ('The Trickster of Seville'). A friar named Gabriel Téllez, who wrote under the pseudonym of Tirso da Molina, there conceived the character and adventures of Don Juan as we know him.

Byron's hero seems to resemble his original only in his name and in his sequence of love encounters. There are, however, some important underlying connections between them that we will discover as the poem unfolds, so it is useful to know something of the original Don Juan story. In the marvellous old play, Don Juan Tenorio is a corrupt nobleman in Seville who seduces women and immediately abandons them. His life repeats the simple sequence of trickery, seduction and flight over and over again. He is detected early in the play by the Commander of Seville, outraged father of a woman whom he has tried to seduce, and kills him in a duel. At the end of the play, after many travels, Juan returns to Seville and takes sanctuary in the church where the Commander is buried. Here, with typical bravado, he invites the stone statue of the Commander to a meal with him. To Juan's surprise the statue takes up the invitation and invites Juan, in turn, to a banquet with him in his tomb. Juan, refusing to be a coward, takes up the invitation, but the ghost of stone grasps Juan's hand and takes him to hell for ever.

This story, clearly, is concerned with sexuality, escape, quick-witted trickery, defiance and judgement. Its hero is a villain but, as with many villains, we have a sneaking sympathy for his reversal of conventional values. Tirso da Molina did not romanticize him, and the audience's horror at Juan's behaviour is confirmed by the religious horror of its conclusion, but it is easy to see how Juan could be romanticized. Don Juan became, like Faust, something of a European folk figure. Molière wrote a play and Mozart wrote an opera (*Don Giovanni*) based upon his exploits. Everybody knew the story through pantomime representation. It is unlikely that Byron had seen the original play, though he may have done so, but he would certainly have been familiar with the basic structure of the Don Juan story and seen versions of it. The nineteenth century produced many versions of the Don Juan story in which he becomes increasingly psychologized as a prototype of Romantic restlessness, and the religious underpinning of the fable is largely lost. Consequently the stone guest and Juan's final damnation begin to disappear from the sequence.

Byron's great poem is written at the moment when the Don Juan story is turning from play into tale and from a judgement upon a libertine into a celebration of liberty. We would expect Byron to use the story to express sympathy for liberty and love but also to convey strong doubts about their possibility and even their value. We would expect him to use it too for a largely satirical account of the various countries and levels of society through which Don Juan travels. All these we find. However, if we take seriously Byron's intolerable awareness of death, suffering, mutability and doubt, we might also expect some kind of religious dimension in his poem. We find this as well and it is far more pervasive than in Molière's or Mozart's versions of the story. What we do not expect is the boldness with which Byron turns his Don Juan into the one who is seduced, makes women his seducers, and thus makes the whole sequence more like an outrageous comedy than a tragedy of damnation. At the same time Byron retains the wastes of suffering, indifference, and death that mark the passage of his Juan just as much as Tirso da Molina's. Byron takes advantage of the indefinite number of Don Juan's seductions to extend his poem into an apparently endless account of life and love in modern Europe.

But we must not be drawn too far into the poem as yet. We have mentioned some of the major influences on the action of the poem and its double-focus structure, but what are the sources of the independent narrator who is at least as important as Juan in Byron's version of the story?

The narrator certainly owes something to eighteenth-century satire. In Swift's *Gulliver's Travels*, for instance, Gulliver is placed in four different societies; these are sometimes satirized via his naïve response to them and sometimes he is himself the object of satire. Byron's narrator is more sophisticated than Gulliver and does not have adventures but, through Juan, he can comment directly or with his tongue in his cheek on the various societies through which Juan passes. Similarly, the narrator's stance as one who writes fearlessly in defence of common sense and moral values in a corrupt and hypocritical world was already fashioned by Alexander Pope in his satires. The narrator is, however, influenced in a contrary direction by the eighteenth-century novelist Laurence Sterne who, in *Tristram Shandy*, constantly draws attention to the fictional nature of his work and to the author's actual process of writing words down on the page. Another thread, different from either of these, is that of the plain historian who describes events simply as occurrences seen from a distance. Byron loved history and read histories of all kinds throughout his life.

We could pursue these precedents further, but they already help us to distinguish the good sense, moral stance, self-consciousness, steady gaze and fluent intimacy with the reader that characterize the narrator of *Don Juan*. We should add one further strand to these. The narrator is greatly preoccupied with doubt, uncertainty and death. When things go wrong in the story, they seem to confirm the narrator's emphasis on the futility of human concerns. When things go right, the narrator often interrupts events in order to remind us of the brief and deceptive nature of human happiness. Drama, philosophy and religion are the three declared sources for this feature of the poem. Shakespeare, of course, often interjects darker registers into comic sequences. Jaques in *As You Like It* is the most obvious example. But Hamlet seems wholly formed of this register. He is fashioned from uncertainty, self-doubt and scorn of others, distrust of sexual instinct and preoccupation with death. The narrator's frequent references to *Hamlet* (and to *Macbeth*) clearly disclose this part of his ancestry. Byron's acquaintance with sceptical philosophy, both classical and European, fashions much of the vocabulary and the settled lack of intellectual conviction of the narrator. Finally Byron's narrator is influenced directly by the Bible, particularly by 'Solomon's' wisdom in Ecclesiastes, and by the critique of human folly fashioned by religious thought in general. One of Byron's favourite poems was Samuel Johnson's *Vanity of Human Wishes*, which was based literarily on a Roman satire by Juvenal but, in spirit, relies on biblical motifs and Christian sentiment. This strain in the narrator's thought suggests darker undercurrents in his customary flippancy and makes his interjections into the sequence of Juan's love-encounters resemble those of Don Juan's servant in the old Spanish play, who constantly reminds the Don, in the midst of his present pleasures, of eventual damnation.

All these influences and models come from Byron's reading or attendance at the theatre. But Byron's own compositions written before and during the appearance of *Don Juan* influence it too. Throughout his life he wrote a vast number of letters that are amongst the most brilliant of any single correspondence. Byron establishes in these, especially in the letters written from the Continent to his English publishers and to various friends, a style that assails his readers with humour, charm, anecdote and dazzling transitions. Obviously the narrator's intimate relationship with the reader and many of his tricks of the trade are based on Byron's letter-writing habits. It is a mistake to press this resemblance too far, however, as some critics have done. The diction and sentence construction of Byron's poem differ significantly from his prose style. It is important, nevertheless, that Byron uses customary speech and conversational habits as one of the sources of his style in *Don Juan*, for many of Byron's contemporaries, Keats for example, try to separate the language of verse from that of ordinary life. Byron wants to blend together or juxtapose humorously the resources of his reading and of his speech, not to separate them.

None of Byron's other poems is directly comparable to *Don Juan*, but *Childe Harold's Pilgrimage* resembles it in scale and endlessness, *Beppo* and *The Vision of Judgement* in verse form, the Oriental tales in some of the settings and subject-matter, and his dramas in the management of episodes. The relationship of *Beppo* to the tales has been outlined earlier and holds good for *Don Juan*. We should emphasize again that, although the management of *ottava rima* stanzas in *Beppo* is the foundation of *Don Juan*'s style and manner, we should not see this as a wholly new beginning; nor should we separate the three poems written in *ottava rima* – *Don Juan*, *The Vision of Judgement* and *Beppo* – from the rest of his achievement. *Beppo* is particularly important because it reminds us that Byron wrote *Don Juan* in Italy and that he spoke and read Italian. He translated part of Dante's *Divine Comedy* and, while writing Cantos III and IV of *Don Juan*, translated Canto I of Pulci's *Morgante Maggiore*, a fifteenth-century poem in *ottava rima* that mixes romance, farce, satire and religion in a way common in Italian but, until Byron, quite unexpected in English poetry. Italian poets like Pulci clearly helped Byron to fashion the new idiom of *Don Juan*, yet again this is not a complete shift in his verse.

Childe Harold's Pilgrimage (1812, 1816, 1818), Byron's other long poem, confirms this. The space available in this short introduction to Byron's poetry does not allow a full discussion of *Childe Harold*, but it is very helpful to know something about it and it is more useful to read *Childe Harold's Pilgrimage* as a preparation for understanding *Don Juan* than any other poem or critical book, even this one. Byron began writing *Don Juan* almost as soon as he had finished *Childe Harold*. We will not attempt to outline the poem here. It is a far more difficult poem for most modern readers to get to grips with than *Don Juan*, although it is well worth the effort. There are four main ways, however, in which *Childe*

Harold sheds positive light on *Don Juan* and one in which it does so negatively.

If we try to see some of the reasons for Byron's choice of style in *Childe Harold*, for instance, *Don Juan* emerges as part of a consistent line of poetic thinking. *Childe Harold* is a long poem written in nine-line rhyming stanzas called 'Spenserian' after the Elizabethan poet Edmund Spenser, who invented them for his famous long poem *The Faerie Queene*. Spenser invented this stanza as an English equivalent of that used by the great Italian poet Ariosto and his predecessors. The plot thickens at this point, for Ariosto's stanza was the very eight-lined *ottava rima* that Byron eventually adopted for *Don Juan*, but which he was not, presumably, prepared to chance at this stage, for it had been used only rarely in English.

Spenser's stanza had, in fact, been imitated by several eighteenth-century poets in semi-comic ways and the style was therefore associated with a rather coy, old-world manner quite different in character from the mainstream verse forms (heroic couplets, blank verse, heroic quatrains) of standard eighteenth-century practice. Byron wanted this calculatedly antique effect for his own poem. He could use it for new or daringly revived effects while, at the same time, protecting himself from charges of excess or bad taste by passing the whole thing off if necessary as clever parody. A modern reader is unlikely to detect this, for the Romantics have taught us to be very earnest about poetry. A ballad such as Coleridge's *Ancient Mariner* was written in much the same way. What Byron wanted to do displays far more shrewdness and insight into verse tradition than he is often given credit for. He picks up a hint from James Beattie, the author of a then well-known poem in Spenserian stanzas called *The Minstrel*, and declares in his preface to *Childe Harold* that Spenser's stanza could be used not only for the quaint and dreamy atmosphere with which it was firmly associated, but for the whole range of effects that Beattie claimed for it ('droll or pathetic, descriptive or sentimental, tender or satirical, as the humour strikes me'). Even at this early stage Byron understood that Spenser's ambition to produce a verse form that could adopt any tone or subject-matter was derived from the practice of Italian poets like Ariosto. Byron wanted to restore the Spenserian stanza so that it was much more like the Italian stanza than was then dreamt of. When the first two cantos of *Childe Harold* were presented to the publisher, they contained strikingly Gothic descriptions of nature, ruins, spectacles and tombs in the manner forged by eighteenth-century practice, but they also contained satirical descriptions of a London Sunday, political cartoons and irreverent speculation. Many of these stanzas were, in fact, cut out at the request of Byron's publishers and friends who did not want their elevated reactions interrupted by good sense or low humour. When Byron came to write the next two cantos of his poem, he abandoned his experiment of a poem mixing different modes in a medley fashion and produced a wholly 'Romantic' poem. This resumé shows clearly that Byron's later choice of *ottava rima*, the original stanza that lay behind Spenser's practice, for *Don Juan* is not a sudden shift of direction but a fresh attempt, with different subject-matter, to find an appropriate style for a medley poem that can be adjusted 'as the humour strikes'.

Childe Harold, like *Don Juan*, is a poem of open form and endless extent. It was begun in 1809. Two cantos appeared in 1812, a third in 1816, and the whole poem was republished with Canto IV in 1818. Byron then turned to *Don Juan*, produced in similar fits and starts, but during the last months of his life in Greece he thought about adding another canto to *Childe Harold*. It is unfinished in this sense. Movement, repetition and development without a final term characterize both poems. Only Byron's death could put a full stop to them. Byron did not always write like this, for his tragedies and tales are governed by their definite conclusions. *Childe Harold* is, therefore, formally a prototype of *Don Juan* and it is not surprising that it helps us to see how to read the later poem.

Childe Harold works on a vast scale, setting one large sequence against another. Harold, like Juan, moves from country to country. A description of Delphi or the Parthenon may be juxtaposed with an account of the wild dancing of Greek brigands, melancholy introspection interrupted by a *tour de force* about the field of Waterloo; or a reaction to the Alps compared with a response to St Peter's basilica in Rome. One of the reasons it is harder to read than *Don Juan* is that there is no narrative thread binding it together and many of its standard allusions are no longer standard for modern readers. We are not supposed, however, merely to react to each of its sections as though they were independent pages in a travel brochure. When, for instance, Byron momentarily compares the Alps with St Peter's, he is activating one of the poem's basic concerns. Which is the better appeaser of human suffering, Nature (the Alps) or art (St Peter's)? And if the answer is art (and in *Childe Harold* it is), then how can we be sure that art is not the human invention

75

of a superior world that does not in fact exist? Its consolations in this case would be seen as an irritant based on illusion. Questions like these are raised by putting one section of the poem against another, for Byron's imagination always works like this. Once this is seen, we will approach *Don Juan* in exactly the same way and set Juan's adventures as a Turkish slave alongside his metaphorical slavery to passion, or see connections as well as distinctions between the worlds of love and war as described in the poem.

When we read *Childe Harold* and *Don Juan* in this way, we are turning them into huge pictures or designs and establishing contrasts or pairings across whole poems; however, as the word 'pilgrimage' implies, *Childe Harold's Pilgrimage* contains forward movement of a kind that pictures by themselves cannot suggest. So we need this perspective as well. Byron's thrilling account of the experience of entering St Peter's in Rome (*Childe Harold*, IV, 154–9) is often invoked to describe the process of reading Byron's poetry. As we move into it, poem or building 'increases' with our advance and the vastness that we encounter is therefore a 'Vastness which grows'. In this way it is 'musical in its immensities', for music, unlike a visual image, involves time and cannot be held in the mind all at once. Nevertheless music suggests some harmonization, cadence or containment of the energies that it sets in motion. Both *Childe Harold* and *Don Juan* change as they proceed. Neither of them simply sets up a programme that is carried out or a pattern that can be repeated exactly. Both poems take chances and risks. Both improve as they proceed. If neither attains a conclusion or is easy to pin down, it would still be a mistake to think of them as getting nowhere or merely advertising different possibilities to their readers.

So the style, procedure, character and development of *Childe Harold* give us a direct purchase on *Don Juan* and help us to read it properly. The narrative line of *Don Juan* and the descriptions and constant historical references of *Childe Harold* make it harder for us to acknowledge their 'imagined lives' than in more obviously 'made-up' poems such as Coleridge's *Ancient Mariner* or Keats's *Hyperion*, but Byron's long poems exist because they were imagined in a particular way, even though Byron always wants to unite the world that we make up and the world that we are given. It is probably easier for us to see the 'imagined life' of *Childe Harold* than that of *Don Juan*, which is too often seen as a realistic and cynical exposure of Romantic imagination. In fact, a correct reading of *Childe Harold* will open our eyes to the same procedures in *Don Juan*.

Nevertheless the two poems remain very different. Byron's great contemporary Goethe used the word 'polarities' to describe opposing poles in human affairs which, as in the physical universe, set up tensions and release energies but maintain a single life because they are equally balanced. *Childe Harold* embodies the opposite polarity to *Don Juan* and, since it is exactly complementary, sheds considerable light on it. For example, Byron sees Europe and Ottoman societies historically in *Childe Harold*. Such histories are made up of wars that produce ruin and ruins, but these historical societies also produced artworks that express the immortal powers of endurance possible to the human mind. History, war and art are produced by a tragic, male consciousness that superintends where it can superintend and endures where it cannot. *Don Juan*, however, although set back thirty years in time, bypasses history and is in love with the present moment. It celebrates social life and natural life, both of which are superintended and symbolized by women. Woman's superintendence has much less outline to it than the male ordering of *Childe Harold*, for women are in league with chance and instinct rather than trying to overcome them. Don Juan himself surrenders to chance and instinct and is therefore attracted by women and attractive to them. At one stage in the poem he almost becomes a woman.

Similarly, *Childe Harold* takes art very seriously. Nature in Canto III cannot heal Byron/Harold's woes. The great cities of Venice and Rome in Canto IV fare a great deal better, for they have almost transformed pitiable human life into superhuman images of ideal grandeur in the midst of decay. The Byron who wrote Canto IV of *Childe Harold* believed in art far more deeply than the Keats who wote 'Ode on a Grecian Urn'. But *Don Juan* will have none of this. Instead of the achieved tragic images of classical art celebrated in *Childe Harold*, *Don Juan* offers us that image of art as process that has become so fashionable in the twentieth century. We are perpetually reminded that the poem is being improvised, that it is, as it were, out of the author's control. Instead of standing apart from the chaos of life and clarifying it for us like a Greek statue, it mimics and endorses the hurly burly of events that evade all our attempts to explain, control or understand them.

Comparisons like this could be extended, for at every point *Childe Harold* throws the opposite assumptions of *Don Juan* into clear relief. We should not make the elementary error of seeing *Don Juan* as Byron's later and better thought on Life and Art that discredits and displaces

77

Childe Harold. Both poems are conceived out of essentially the same world view but represent the opposed polarities that keep it in place. Tragedy and comedy are the traditional names for these polarities and we should side with the early nineteenth-century commentator John Wilson Croker who wrote, 'I am agreeably disappointed at finding *Don Juan* very little offensive. It is by no means worse than *Childe Harold* which it resembles as Comedy does Tragedy.'

Finally, it is helpful to look at *Don Juan* in the light of Byron's dramas. Byron's dramatic poem *Manfred* was published in 1817 before *Don Juan* was begun, but his major dramas, *Marino Faliero, Sardanapalus, The Two Foscari* and *Cain*, were written in 1820–21, for the most part during the sixteen months when the writing of *Don Juan* was suspended (between Cantos V and VI).

These dramas are elevated, concentrated and austere. They are serious plays in verse that manage to escape from Shakespeare's shadow. They proceed from Byron's 'self-denying ordinance to dramatize, like the Greeks . . . striking passages of history' (letter to Murray, 14 July 1821). In structure they are more like French classical theatre than English drama. In their subject-matter – political ideas and the opposition of male and female attitudes to social order – they resemble the plays of Ibsen. On the whole they have been little read, but recent criticism has taken them very seriously indeed and those who do read them are impressed.

Clearly these tragic plays stand apart from *Don Juan* rather than complement it like *Childe Harold.* They help us to see two important points, however. Byron, for a variety of reasons, avoided Shakespeare's dramatic influence in his plays, though he was more intimately acquainted with Shakespeare's text and stage performance than most English poets. Classical theatre produces concentrated effects by eliminating as much as it can. Shakespeare, on the contrary, loves to construct different worlds – think of *A Midsummer Night's Dream* or *The Tempest* – and forces his audience to make rapid adjustments from dukes to tradesmen, faeries, pastoral lovers with Greek names and donkey-headed braggarts. He forces us also to see connections and parallels between these different worlds. Shakespeare's influence, kept out from Byron's plays, breaks out in the comic texture and constant adjustments of tone in *Don Juan.* But Byron's dramatic expertise is evident in its own right and plays an important part in *Don Juan.* The original story of *Don Juan* is found in a play. Dramatic narratives can cut from one scene to another and make us attend to ironies of sequence much more vividly than a novel which, normally, supplies all the connecting bits so that we 'feel' the sequence but do not attend to it. Attending to a sequence is precisely what Byron's poem and the old Spanish Don Juan play are concerned to bring about, and Byron therefore uses dramatic techniques much more than is customary in novels or even in most narrative poems. It is no good asking for the story of Byron's *Don Juan* or, thwarted there, looking only at the characters. These questions, in that order usually, work for most novels, although, of course, modern critics are always trying to make us ask questions that seem more sophisticated than these. In the same way there is little value in concentrating upon the story or the characters in *A Midsummer Night's Dream*. They are there, but they cannot be our main interest.

We have spent some time circling *Don Juan* like this because catching the influences and sources that shape the poem helps us to avoid patronizing or simplifying it, and assists us to read it in the right way. But the range of modes that Byron fuses together is a reliable indication of his mental energy and abundant genius. J. Livingstone Lowes wrote a famous book on Coleridge called *The Road to Xanadu* (1927 and still in print). In this book he tried to demonstrate how Coleridge's imagination assimilated all kinds of odd bits of reading and information that he had gathered together, for the most part unconsciously, over the years. The book is a brilliant piece of detective work, but many now argue that the evidence it presents can be read differently and tells us more about twentieth-century views on imagination than about Romantic poetry. Coleridge, though formidably well read, undoubtedly faked some of his learning, and intended some of his erudition and, more surprisingly, his 'unconscious' process to be lauded and unearthed. We cannot take sides in this dispute here, but the issue of whether great writers, especially poets, know what they are doing is bound up with *Don Juan* itself, for *Don Juan* was written at a time when the processes of the imagination were beginning to be preferred to its finished products. Certainly accidents and the deep intertwining of buried memories are responsible for some of the most profound effects in writing literature, though poets, for the most part, do not write in a trance. The most exciting characteristic of poetry is the way in which lucidity and full consciousness seem to give and take life from hidden tracks of mental space, forgotten histories, unutterable rhythms. *Don Juan* shows us a poet trusting to chance more than most, rhyming his way gleefully into a future that he cannot penetrate and yet, at the same time, the poet here is one who, consciously not unconsciously, juxtaposes, fuses and deploys all the central traditions of thought, words and feeling that come down to him and sets them steadily in a new order.

To conclude this section we must briefly set out the major themes of *Don Juan*. This should be a simple matter, but it is harder than it looks, for one of its main themes is the many connections both obvious and obscure, between apparently different things. If, for instance, we isolate four major concerns of the poem – love, liberty, knowledge and poetry itself – it is clear that the first three are often inextricable. *Don Juan*, for example, is awakened in adolescence both to knowledge as such and to sexual knowledge. 'Philosophy' and 'puberty' merge (I, 93). Similarly, Catherine the Great in Canto IX is an emblem of sexual passion, which is there seen as a form of tyranny closely bound up with political tyranny. Love itself is shown to be bound up with politics, social patterns, nature, male and female psychology, sin and paradise. Love therefore cannot be a distinct topic bracketed off from the other concerns of the poem. However, we can say that it is the main focus of the narrative at least until the Siege in Canto VII, largely disappears from the poem in Cantos X–XII and re-emerges in the final cantos.

Knowledge, similarly, is a constant pre-occupation of the narrator and moves centre-stage in Cantos X–XII, where Love is ousted from the poem. By 'knowledge' here we mean the narrator's obsession with doubt and certainty and, more generally, the habits of reflection and generalization that the narrator brings to the instinctive and accident-prone adventures of Juan. Knowledge primarily engages the narrator's mind, but there is what we now call an existentialist bias to his thinking too. 'Existentialism' was a dominant form of philosophical thinking on the Continent in the mid years of this century. Byron was (via Nietzsche) undoubtedly one of the progenitors of this form of thinking. Byron's narrator may be called 'existentialist' in that his thinking involves and presupposes his own existence, especially insofar as he knows that he is a being who is going to die. The narrator's preoccupation with doubt and certainty is closely bound up with his awareness of death, for it is the whole person and not just the mind that enters the unknown territory of death.

'Liberty' as a theme belongs both to the events of the narrative and to the narrator's comments. Juan embodies freedom in his avoidance of planning and in his refusal to submit to anyone other than a pretty woman. The narrator normally voices Byron's own liberal political sentiments about post-Napoleonic Europe and about the pre-revolution societies through which Juan moves.

Liberty is not an unqualified absolute in *Don Juan*, however. We see this clearly when we consider Byron's views on poetry. Poetry itself is a theme in this work in two ways. First of all, *Don Juan* is directed against then new theories of poetry that emphasized originality and imagination above all else and promoted obscurity. Hence Byron lambasts Southey in his ironic dedication to the Poet Laureate and attacks Wordsworth, Coleridge, Keats and others. *Don Juan*, in contrast, is set forth as a public, intelligible poem grounded in precedents ('Thou shalt believe in Milton, Dryden, Pope', I, 205). Secondly, *Don Juan* always indicates that it is what it appears to be: a poem that depends upon the ceaseless invention of Byron and the use of conventions and clichés, however ironical the poem is about these things. The poem is thus shown as emerging from the free inspiration of the moment, it is itself 'liberal' in this way, but at the same time it is not trying to escape from good sense or the established procedures of great poetry.

When we talk in this second way about the theme of poetry in *Don Juan*, we are no longer picturing a theme as a thread or constant object of attention in the poem but as something that participates in its dynamism. This is true of all the 'themes' in the poem. *Don Juan* does have definite areas of concern, but the poem is not merely the means by which Byron speaks his mind about this or that. *Don Juan* is a very odd poem, for it has a life of its own which, nevertheless, seems to catch directly the processes of life and thought that lie outside it. For instance, the energies of sexual love and the strange blankness out of which our thoughts spring are not only talked about in *Don Juan*, they are mimicked and, in some strange way, contained within it. Every reader notices the 'life' of the poem. Byron himself wrote of it, 'is it not *life*, is it not the *thing*?' (letter to Kinnaird, 26 October 1818). That is one reason why, however necessary selected editions are, it is essential to read the whole of the poem if we are to understand it. The first four cantos, for example, mean something different when taken with the remaining twelve. *Don Juan* does not just 'go on'. It grows. The best way of keeping track of the themes is to stay as close as we can to the unfolding episodes of the poem.

Episodes

Dedication

Don Juan is preceded by a prose preface and a verse dedication. The preface makes fun of Wordsworth's own preface to the *Lyrical Ballads*, and the dedication savages Robert Southey, the Poet Laureate. It was not thought wise to print either of these with the original poem.

In his preface Byron makes elaborate fun of Wordsworth's use of a distinct narrator in his poem 'The Thorn', mocks the banality of some of Wordsworth's attempts to reproduce everyday speech in verse, and implies that *Don Juan*, like Wordsworth's *Lyrical Ballads*, is designed to be a manifesto poem though of a different kind. Byron, like Wordsworth, will use a narrator, but this narrator will not be an elaborately dramatized construction and he will often merge with Byron's own voice. Byron, like Wordsworth, will write plain poetry in a plain style, but he will not deride Pope and Dryden nor despise poetic diction. To make his own intentions and his criticism of Wordsworth clear, Byron puts an epigraph from Horace at the head of *Don Juan: Difficile est proprie communia dicere* ('It is difficult to talk of common things in an appropriate way'). *Don Juan* does just this.

The dedication to Southey is, of course, ironical. Southey, and Wordsworth too in a way, represent the new public taste in poetry which, from Byron's point of view, displaces Pope and Dryden's achievement, accepts banal and unpoetic idioms into verse and authorizes obscurity. At the same time these poets now praise rather than criticize current society. *Don Juan* is designed to do the opposite of all these things:

> Besides, I hate all mystery, and that air
> Of claptrap, which your recent poets prize.
>   (II, 124)

Therefore the ironical dedication to Southey is Byron's way of nailing his colours to the mast at the outset of his poem. Byron is not so much concerned to attack Wordsworth's or Southey's poetry in itself (there are times when he praises both) but to attack their notion of poetry and the poetic practices that they were handing on to others. It is for this reason that Byron praises Scott, Rogers, Campbell, Moore and Crabbe in stanza 7. They are not Byron's choice of the Top Five Poets, but they use what Byron considered to be a serviceable idiom in their poetry. In

Don Juan Byron fashions just such a serviceable idiom. It is a Romantic poem, self-conscious in procedure but about everything under the sun ('Ocean' rather than the 'Lakes' of Wordsworth and Southey). It is deliberately addressed to a common reader, cultured but interested in more than books, rather than to the Romantic insider or the modern critic.

Byron demonstrates his own freedom of allegiance in stanzas 12–16; these attack Viscount Castlereagh, who was Foreign Secretary from 1812–22. Byron had a peculiar horror of Castlereagh. The vituperative energy displayed in these vicious lines is fine in itself, though contempt of this kind is usually tempered in *Don Juan* by a comic detachment that is missing here until Southey once again looms into Byron's sights in the final stanza.

Juan in Seville (Canto I)

The first canto establishes the mode of the poem, introduces us to Juan and the narrator, sketches society in Seville, and describes Juan's first love-affair. The action resembles that of a dramatic farce. The canto is self-contained in a way untypical of the poem's later procedures.

Juan is born in Seville because that is where the original Don Juan comes from, although, unlike his precursor, we learn something of Juan's education. He is sheltered from the society of other boys and his education carefully avoids 'anything that's loose/Or hints continuation of the species' (I, 40). Juan is not allowed to be a boy or to know anything about sexuality. It is ironical, then, and perhaps inevitable, that he remains permanently boyish and his later life is dominated by sexual love.

Juan's mother, Donna Inez, is responsible for this, and her solicitude and hypocritical prudery are seen as typical of Seville and society in general where 'love is taught hypocrisy from youth' (I, 72). Juan's education coincides with his natural growth and development, which supply what his education omits, but he has no idea what is happening to him. Byron makes several points through his comic analysis here (I, 87–97). Although critical of the suppressions in Juan's education, he realizes there is some advantage in unknowingness. Juan's ignorance is comic, but it also guarantees freshness, intensity and innocence in his first love-encounter (and in all subsequent ones up to Catherine the Great). Similarly, Juan's adolescent restlessness and increased awareness of 'himself and the whole earth' (I, 92) are a direct result of puberty (I, 93) and, through this, Byron makes fun of Wordsworth's 'self-communions' by hinting at a similarly displaced sexuality that underlies them. However, Byron is not simply being cynical here. One of the major insistences of the poem is that material, intellectual and spiritual realities are all interconnected in bewildering ways.

Halfway through the canto Byron alters his focus and zooms in upon Don Juan and Julia at half-past six 'on the sixth of June' (I, 104). We are to follow the process of Juan's first love-affair in detail up to, but not including, its consummation. This is a pattern that will be repeated throughout the poem. Julia, a brilliant character-study, is 'married, charming, chaste and twenty-three'. As usual in *Don Juan* we are directed to bring several balancing perspectives to bear on her. She is attractive, vivacious and intelligent ('her veins ran lightning', I, 61). Her husband Don Alfonso, is twice her age and has, very probably, been the lover of Juan's mother before his marriage. We are thus sympathetic to Julia because of the gap between her innate warmth and the tepidity of her married life. Moreover the narrator is at pains to remind us of 'the controlless core/Of human hearts' (I, 116) which, if true, must excuse Julia's indiscretion. Nevertheless where Juan is unknowing about sexual passion,

> There surely will be little doubt with some
> That Donna Julia knew the reason why,
> But as for Juan, he had no more notion
> Than he who never saw the sea of ocean.
>
> (I, 70)

Both Juan and Julia are swept along by natural forces into their love-affair, although Julia's arousal is intensified and modulated by self-consciousness. She is, however sympathetic, a hypocrite (I, 72). She remains conscious of the social, moral and religious laws that she is transgressing even while she pretends to herself that she is keeping them. Her love-affair is, so the poem tells us, wrong, avoidable, inevitable and right.

Immediately upon the lovers' consummation, the narrator produces a long digression (I, 118–36) that distances us from them and gives us the impression of duration in the love-affair. We then zoom in upon a new narrative sequence that will put a full-stop to Julia and force Juan into fresh adventures. The conduct of this episode becomes blatantly farcical, as the stereotypes of jealous husband, quick-witted wife, well-hidden lover and his unfortunately discovered shoes are all played out. The change of tone is important, for laughter here releases us from our attachment to Juan and Julia's tender coupling. Julia suddenly emerges as a magnificently confident hypocrite as she upbraids her husband and proclaims her own fidelity. This scene is in clever contrast to her earlier hypocrisy that she could barely acknowledge to herself. We ourselves accept that the love-affair that seemed so fresh a few stanzas back now belongs to a recognizable stereotype. Similarly, the physical intimacy that then seemed so magical is now made vulgarly comic as Julia, presumably, sits on Juan inside her bed in order to hide him from her husband's searches. But we are in for a further surprise. Julia, soon after Juan's discovery and her disgrace, 'was sent into a nunnery' (I, 191) and, from there, sends Juan a letter (I, 192–8). This letter is modelled upon Pope's much longer 'Eloisa to Abelard' and reveals Julia to us directly. It seems to bypass the narrator and the narrative. In this letter Julia is complex and confused, but she is no longer a hypocrite. She 'cannot regret' her love for Juan and yet acknowledges 'my shame and sorrow'. She produces a famous aphorism that is often quoted as though it were said in Byron's own voice but it belongs to her:

> 'Man's love is of his life a thing apart,
> 'Tis woman's whole existence . . .'
> (I, 194)

She then forecasts correctly Juan's future exploits while 'All is o'er' for her. She 'cannot collect' her mind and is in evident distress; yet, in some contrast to this:

> This note was written upon gilt-edged paper
> With a neat crow quill, rather hard but new.
> (I, 198)

We notice that her 'small white fingers' tremble as she puts her personal seal on the letter, but 'she did not let one tear escape her'. These details take us wonderfully close to Julia's poised yet vulnerable spirit, just as we have been in the account of her wilfully muddled consciousness as she seduces Juan. At other times in Canto I we see her with rapture, as Juan or any lover might, and with the admiration a bystander might feel in the scene with her husband.

An important element in *Don Juan* is this closeness to and sympathy for his characters' feelings. Julia is treated warmly and fairly by Byron. She is an individual who feels, suffers and exists. We prefer her to those who surround her. But she is also a stereotype, a spectacular phenomenon and an artful manipulator of her own and others' feelings.

The capacity to maintain this aesthetic and moral objectivity alongside real sympathy for Julia is the mark of Byron's greatness.

The Shipwreck (Canto II)

Juan survives his first adventure, but Julia's life is paralysed by it. Although we sympathize with Juan as hero and perpetual survivor, in two episodes of the poem (Canto II, Cantos VII–VIII) we set his survival against the deaths of thousands of his companions. The shipwreck scene thus brings to the forefront of our attention what is only an undertone in the first canto.

The shipwreck itself is an accident. It spoils Donna Inez's plan for Juan to 'mend his former morals' by travel in France and Italy. Similarly, Julia's plan of self-control (I, 83), like all plans in *Don Juan*, makes no headway against the forces of Nature and the effects of chance. The poem proceeds, and Juan lives, by accident and chance. Where before we followed closely the sequence of Julia's seduction of Juan and were taken into her confused consciousness, now we enter into the hour-by-hour feelings of the shipwrecked sailors and share their longing for survival.

The will to survive is natural but it is also selfish, and, as in the cannibalism of the famished sailors, may horrify us. In this way Byron forces us to modify the fairly simple opposition that we have relied upon in Canto I between 'society' (i.e. hypocritical Seville) and 'Nature' (i.e. Juan and Julia's love-affair). 'Nature' may not always be beneficent: it can enact destructive patterns in the events of the natural cosmos and in the dark motions of the human will (II, 72). Thus when the sailors turn to cannibalism we are told that

> None in particular had sought or planned it;
> 'Twas nature gnawed them to this resolution,
>
> (II, 75)

The account of the shipwreck uses two very different resonances that are habitual in Byron's poetry. The first of these is fact. Few poets are so anxious as Byron to tether imaginative accounts to factual detail. He wrote to his publisher that 'There should always be some foundation of fact for the most airy fabric and pure invention is but the talent of a liar' (2 April 1817). When the sailors try desperately to pump water out of the sinking ship, we are told that the pumps throw up 'fifty tons of water' per hour and that they were made by 'Mr. Mann of London' (II, 28).

Byron took such details from the travel books that he loved to read. They give these stanzas a bizarre sense of accuracy and curiously intensify the pathos of the sailors' doomed struggle for survival. The second resource is the opposite of the first. Byron loved the Old Testament and had read Dante. His imagination always responds deeply to religious visions of destruction. An unfinished poem of his called *Heaven and Earth*, for instance, gives a superb sense of the terrible energies of destruction released in Noah's Flood. There are several references to the Flood in Canto II (66, 91, 93) and to Dante's account of the horrors of hell (II, 83). Stanza 49 in particular shows us a vision of Night as the masked face of God who hates and condemns mankind, although Byron, characteristically, steps aside from direct statement here and says 'Thus to their hopeless eyes the night was shown'.

This visionary capacity is revealed not only in the scale and intensity of this scene, but also in Byron's capacity to hold on to details. Julia's carefully written letter, for instance, is read by Juan until his attention is suddenly removed by a bout of sea-sickness (II, 19). The detail, though comic, again emphasizes the power of present circumstance and natural accident to disrupt plans for the future and loyalty to the past. The letter turns up again when the sailors are looking for paper to use as lots to decide who is to be eaten first. The ironies here are telling. Similarly, the oar that 'providentially' was put within Juan's grasp, prevents him from drowning and brings him to shore (II, 107, 110) was thrown into the longboat 'by good luck' by 'a young lad' sixty stanzas earlier (II, 48). Again, the corpse that Juan discovers washed up beside him (II, 109) is one of the three at the bottom of the boat in stanza 98.

Keats read these shipwreck stanzas while voyaging to Italy not long before he died and was disgusted by them. We certainly cannot evade the grimness and callousness of parts of this episode. We should remember, however, that shipwrecked sailors do not invariably behave like Gregory Peck and that there is some tenderness and decorum as well as horror shown here. The account of the two fathers and the different deaths of their sons (II, 87–90) is convincingly felt. Even the cannibalism episode is a weird tribute to the retained force of manners that impart a human and social structure to the sailors' 'savage hunger'. Pedrillo (Juan's tutor), having kissed a crucifix, is bled to death by a surgeon who, in turn, is given the blood as his fee. Notwithstanding this strange decorum, all those who eat human flesh go mad and Juan, the only survivor, pointedly refuses to eat.

Juan and Haidée (Cantos II–IV)

From the reader's point of view the transition from Juan's escape from drowning to his awakening by 'A lovely female face of seventeen' (II, 112) is an immediate and sudden reversal of fortune. We notice too the subsequent intensity and immediacy of passion between Juan and Haidée. Byron is at pains, however, to suggest some duration in both.

This can be seen by looking at the structure of the episode, which falls into three distinct sections. In the first of these Juan is awakened from sleep gradually over a period of time ('And thus a moon rolled on', II, 174). This awakening is continually compared to a resurrection from the dead (II, 111–15, 134, 138, 144, 147, 150, 158). As soon as Juan is restored to healthy life, Juan and Haidée become lovers in a bond of natural marriage. This sequence is completed by the end of Canto II (a canto with more incidents than any other in the poem). The second stage takes up the whole of Canto III. It consists of the return of Lambro, Haidée's father, and the description of a meal over which Juan and Haidée preside. The final section (Canto IV up to stanza 75) shows the disruption of the love-idyll and concentrates on the effect of this on Haidée. Her sleep and awakening to madness in this section reverse the opening sequence of Juan's resurrection from drowning and torpor. As can be seen at once, the structure here is both logical and subtle. In Canto IV, for instance, Haidée repeats in a dream the sequence of events that occur in Canto II. Here, however, the shadow-side of that experience emerges. Instead of finding Juan washed up alive, in her dream he is dead. The cave that provided refuge and restoration for Juan is, in her dream, 'hung with marble icicles' and redolent of horror. The sea-shore that had 'shining pebbles' and 'smooth and hardened sand' when the lovers walked along it in Canto II is, in her dream, made of 'sharp shingles' that tear 'her bleeding feet'. Worst of all, as Haidée gazes on the dead face of Juan in her dream, it slowly turns into, and for a moment is identical with, the actual face of her live and accusing father. The patterns inside Haidée's head and in the design of these cantos fuse together.

Other effects, equally brilliant, depend upon separation rather than imaginative fusions. The awakening of Juan and the 'marriage' of the lovers is told in a succession of stanzas that, as with Juan and Julia, stay as close as possible to the sequence that it describes. As soon as this sequence is complete, however, we are given throughout Canto III an altogether different perspective that distances us from the lovers. We suddenly see everything through the eyes of Lambro, who returns, unrecognized, to the daughter and society that have forgotten him. This detaches us from Juan and Haidée, since Lambro's viewpoint is legitimate though disregarded. In another way this device intensifies our concern for the lovers, because Lambro is a threatening presence likely to destroy the world on which he gazes. Byron probably copied Milton's precedent here, for in *Paradise Lost* the innocent paradise of Adam and Eve is described for us always from the perspective of Satan, who has come to destroy it.

In Canto IV we find a further change in narrative. We are again close to the lovers, Lambro is ominously unmentioned and the narrator produces a series of choric comments that tell us the lovers are doomed.

Through these structural patterns and narrative dislocations we are made to react in different ways to the lovers while, simultaneously, we are given a real sense of the duration of their love-affair. This is important in itself because their love is timeless and thus cannot be described in terms of duration. This cliché is made vivid for us by another narrative detail that is deftly embedded in the structure. If we set three stanzas from three different cantos (II, 185; III, 101; IV, 20) alongside one another, we will find Juan and Haidée in all three of the narrative sections gazing at one another and at the glow of sunset that surrounds and lights them. The sunset in Canto II is the backdrop to their first love-making and plainly refers back to and answers the grim vision of the shipwreck when 'the sunless day went down/Over the waste of waters' (II, 49). Now, however, the cosmos appears to be in league with the generation of love rather than with destruction. A canto later, the great feast is over,

> And every sound of revelry expired.
> The lady and her lover, left alone,
> The rosy flood of twilight's sky admired.
> (III, 101)

The vocabulary here takes us straight back to Canto II, 185 ('rosy flood', 'rosy ocean'). It is as though the lovers simply pick up again where they left off or re-enter a permanent and timeless world. When in Canto IV yet again 'They gazed upon the sunset', both lovers sense that this is 'their last day of happy date' and they associate this with the

89

disappearing sun (IV, 22). The sunset in this way comes to represent the 'glow' of their love. 'Glow' is a keyword in Byron's description of love throughout *Don Juan* (see for instance I, 106, 115; V, 117). It signifies the changed and charged consciousness of lovers. It is at once physical (as in blushing) and a declaration of lovers' heightened self-consciousness. When Juan and Haidée are attracted to and bathed in the light of sunset, we are pointed to the force inherent in life itself that promotes sexual attraction, generation and consciousness. The repetition of sunsets suggests the rhythm of sexual love and its repeated and identical ecstasies. Love has no history and escapes from sequence altogether. Sunset also suggests, however, closure and proximity to ending. It is the gateway to the night of lovers, but it is also the end of light. In this way Byron suggests at once the timeless and the time-bound character of Juan and Haidée's love. Similar paradoxes characterize Haidée, Lambro and the society built round the lovers in Canto III. We can take each of these in turn.

Haidée is the most fully realized of all Byron's heroines and engages all our sympathy. The one essential thing to say about Juan and Haidée's idyll is that it presents human love with authenticity and warmth. English literature in comparison with, for example, Italian or Russian literature is surprisingly deficient in convincing and enthusiastic accounts of sexual passion. Byron's portrait of Juan and Haidée and Shakespeare's Romeo and Juliet are magnificent exceptions to this generalization. We need to state this clearly at the outset and hang on to it, despite the fact that Byron plants some unmistakable qualifications of the lovers in his account. For instance, Haidée's eyes are 'black as death' and their glance is like an arrow's flight or the attack of a poisonous snake (II, 117). She mothers and possesses Juan. Her small mouth seems 'almost prying into his for breath' (II, 113) and she is compared to a mother bird visiting Juan 'in his nest' (II, 168). She is 'Nature's bride' and 'Passion's child' (II, 202), but she also wears make-up (III, 75), jewellery and Turkish trousers (III, 72). Her brow, similarly, is 'overhung with coins of gold' (II, 116). These derive, presumably, from her father's piracy upon which her wealth and position as 'princess' of the island depend. Byron casually reminds us that 'Haidée forgot the island was her sire's' (III, 13). Anyone familiar with Byron's mind will detect enormous resonances in this line, for, although Byron is always sympathetic to those who try to break out of the inherited cycle of guilt, suffering and injustice that forms human history, he thinks that it is impossible to do so. Haidée is Juan's bride but remains Lambro's daughter:

> Her father's blood before her father's face
> Boiled up and proved her truly of his race.
> (IV, 44)

Ultimately her father is Adam and there are constant references to the Fall of Man in these cantos. Haidée forgets not only her father and her kinship with crime, but also about the consequent punishments of hell and purgatory 'Just in the very crisis she should not' (II, 193). There are more references of this kind and we may be surprised to note this insistence, but we should still maintain our enthusiasm for Juan and Haidée's mutual love 'after nature's fashion' (II, 191).

Lambro's return and the love-feast in Canto III are designed to unsettle our enthusiasm rather more. Lambro is an engaging and complex character based on the Byronic heroes of the Oriental tales, though here he is a father rather than a lover. He belongs, as they do, to a world of pain, memory, thwarted idealism (III, 54), leadership, prudence and action. The tenderness that other Byronic heroes have for women is here concentrated on Lambro's daughter (II, 57). His focus, like Juan's and the reader's, is on Haidée, although the pattern of experience that he brings to bear is quite different. He does not advertise his feelings, but his 'strong human heart' is pained and maddened by Haidée's desertion of his memory (III, 57–8). In the end, and it is a compelling, tragic irony, he does reclaim her. She behaves as his daughter ('How like they looked', IV, 44) and, finally, the two remain together and alone, entombed on the 'desolate, and bare' island that once seemed to be paradise.

The love-feast is, in the first instance, a natural extension of Juan and Haidée's love. Nurtured in secret and consummated before 'The silent ocean and the starlight bay' (II, 188), it yet becomes the foundation of a society and results in a child (IV, 70). Their intimacy is physical, psychological, natural, social and procreative. It is a new creation and revolutionary in its social implications. Lambro's isle of prudence (money-hoarding) and guilt is transformed into a festival of food and love. But it is not only Lambro's disenchanted eye that doubts the solidity of this enchanted isle. The narrator suggests that the isle represents both 'innocent desires' and 'illicit Indulgence' (III, 13). The lovers are surrounded, worryingly, by 'work of splendour . . . Gazelles

and cats/And dwarfs and blacks . . . As plentiful as in a court or fair'
(III, 68). They do not eat al fresco with the others, but have an inner
room of their own in which they sit enthroned 'in their beauty and their
pride' (III, 61). Above all, as they sit in luxury, dressed in Turkish
costume, their entertainment includes a song, 'The Isles of Greece', which
upbraids their whole way of life and love's indifference to perspectives
other than pleasure's. This song, one of Byron's best lyrics and often
anthologized separately, functions like the writing on the wall in Bel-
shazzar's feast (Byron makes the point in III, 65) to suggest a different
morality and a coming destruction. Momentarily, Juan and Haidée seem
ignoble slaves of passion confined in a 'bowre of blisse' like those in
which the ancient heroes of epic and romance are momentarily detained
(Ulysses on Calypso's isle; Aeneas in Dido's Carthage; Rinaldo in
Armida's bower). The ease and efficiency with which Lambro and his
men resume control of the island (IV, 47) suggest the superficiality of
the changes that love has brought about there.

It must be emphasized that Juan and Haidée's love is positively represented in the poem, although the contrary indications assembled here
show how complex and delicate is Byron's handling of this idyll. These
inescapable qualifications should not undermine our enthusiasm for the
lovers; in a way they increase it because we take into account these
perspectives and values, which human love tends to omit or slight.

If, however, our sympathy is so much engaged for Juan's love and
Haidée's fate, how can we be manoeuvred into maintaining interest in
what comes next? This is a real problem for Byron and he solves it with
the utmost directness. Juan is knocked on the head and dispatched to a
slave-ship. Haidée goes mad and dies, and wonderful tribute is paid to
her; hence

> But let me change this theme, which grows too sad,
>> And lay this sheet of sorrows on the shelf.
> I don't much like describing people mad,
>> For fear of seeming rather touched myself.

(IV, 74)

Juan now suddenly 'found himself at sea'. He is dulled by the pain of
his head wound and stimulated by new sights and sounds so that he
cannot 'altogether call the past to mind' (IV, 75). The effect is brutal,
convincing and comic. We are shocked but we laugh and, in doing so,
accept our severance from Haidée's island. What we thus do explicitly
and with laughter is supported by all kinds of less obvious symbols and

indicators. The sea, for instance, is again being used to symbolize death and resurrection, forgetfulness and restoration, as it is so often in comedy and romance adventure. Juan's ship, en route to Constantinople, sails 'six knots an hour before the wind' past the ruins of Troy and the tombs of ancient epic heroes (IV, 75–9). Juan, forlorn and 'Weak still with loss of blood', comes on deck and contemplates 'many a hero's grave'. The important thing here is that Juan, weak but already recovering health, is not one of these heroes. Haidée's grave is left behind him. The poem too is about what happens beyond such tragic end-points as the death of Haidée. In this sense the comparison with Shakespeare's last comedies – full of renewals, sea imagery and written after his tragedies – is a precise one and the point is underlined by Byron himself. Haidée, for instance, just before her death, is like one 'who championed human fears' (IV, 43). This is a phrase that Byron used earlier of Manfred, his tragic hero. She is compared in her deathlike sleep to the three heroic sculptures that Byron apostrophizes at the end of *Childe Harold* (IV, 61). When she dies, like Macbeth 'she sleeps well' (IV, 71). When, however, Juan wakes up, another allusion to *Macbeth* describes him as 'cabined, cribbed, confined' (IV, 75). The pun on 'cabined' is atrocious and funny; hence the tragic allusion is now made to look ridiculous. These references to the sea, epic heroes and Shakespearian tragedy could not be more specific or exactly placed. They reveal the magnitude of Byron's ambition in this engagingly modest poem. The easiest way to select from *Don Juan* is to anthologize the first four cantos. Many readers therefore get no farther than this. Any reading is better than no reading, but *Don Juan* is about what happens beyond tragedy and beyond Haidée's isle.

What immediately happens to Juan in the last section of Canto IV is that a troupe of Italian singers, held captive with Juan on the slave-ship, surround our comic hero with a tangle of gossip and reminiscence, just as Laura does to Beppo. In this way Juan is prevented from maintaining loyalty to the past much as sea-sickness interrupts his faithful reading of Julia's letter. Our worst fear is that Juan will forget Haidée. He does not immediately do so, but, when we see him actually chained to an attractive Italian brunette (IV, 92–5), we find his resistance to her charms a matter for absurd comedy. It is not Juan's propensity or weakness for women that endanger him so much as the unpredictable accidents which, after all, took him to Haidée's isle in the first place. No plan for the future or shaped memory of the past can hold out against the clamour of particular, unforeseen sights and sounds for long.

The Harem (Cantos V–VI)

In the next episode Juan is taken to the slave-market in Constantinople where we find him, vividly described, among the 'shivering slaves' on 'a raw day of autumn's bleak beginning' (V, 6). He is bought by Baba, a black eunuch, on behalf of the capricious Sultana Gulbeyaz, who has spotted him 'in passing on his way to sale' (V, 114). In order to hide him from the Sultan, he is brought to the Sultana disguised as a harem girl, but he refuses to make love to her because he is ordered to do so and still cannot forget Haidée (V, 124). The Sultan arrives to spend the night with Gulbeyaz and Juan is returned to the harem with the other concubines and wives. Still in disguise, he shares a bed with Dudù, one of the harem girls. This enrages Gulbeyaz who, the following morning, gives orders that Juan and Dudù should be drowned in a sack in the Bosphorus. Canto VI ends in uncertainty as to what happens and the beginning of Canto VII switches abruptly to a different location altogether. This, in brief, is what happens in Cantos V and VI. What are Byron's purposes in these cantos?

Clearly he wants to change the scene and characters of the poem after Haidée's isle, while, as usual, establishing some links with the previous episode. Juan and Haidée were, in a way, slaves of passion. Their manners and costume belonged to that of the Turkish overlords of Greece and Juan's new position as a slave in a Turkish harem, emasculated in appearance and chosen plaything of the Sultana, is a worrying travesty of his former role. The metaphor of slavery to passion and to whims of all kinds ('Most men are slaves', V, 25) is deployed thoughtfully in this section. The other main theme is, once again, Nature. Sexuality, though part of Nature, often urges us to distort it. The problematic relationship between gender and sexuality is a particular focus here. As a story-teller Byron's principal problem is to engage us with a further love-adventure while, at the same time, allowing the special emotions generated by Haidée and her death to retain some force.

The episode relies upon broad contrasts and intricate connections. The first are the easier to describe. Juan, for instance, pairs up with Johnson, an English slave, who is also bought by Baba. Johnson is masculine, shrewd and disillusioned with love and other human 'rainbows', but he remains cheerful (V, 21–2). He makes an evident contrast with Juan and, in some ways, resembles the narrator of the poem. He is 'A man of thirty' (V, 10). Byron was thirty-two when he composed Johnson's portrait.

The Sultan's palace is in distinctly characterized sections. The State rooms and Sultana's apartment (Canto V) are splendid but soulless and inhabited by mutes, eunuchs and dwarfs. They represent, on a vaster scale, what worried us in the account of Juan and Haidée's feast (III, 68–78) and are blatantly unnatural. Juan's disguise as a girl and the Sultana's masculine instigation of passion ('A poniard decked her girdle', V, 111) form part of these reverses of Nature. The harem itself (Canto VI) is quite other than this. Where the Sultana's boudoir has porcelain vases with 'fettered flowers' (VI, 97), the ladies of the harem once inside their own quarters are themselves 'Like flowers of different hue and clime and root' (VI, 65). They seem unfettered, like 'birds' or 'waves at spring tide' or 'women anywhere/When freed from bonds' (VI, 34). It is not surprising, therefore, that Juan, who refuses to be constrained to love in the Sultana's apartment, takes advantage of his disguise within the harem to make love to Dudù, the 'child of Nature' (VI, 60) with whom he is paired. She, unlike the Sultana, is 'a soft landscape of mild earth', unself-conscious, 'quiet', 'serene' and 'serious' (VI, 53–4). The contrast with the Sultana is evident, but Byron handles Juan and Dudù's encounter with considerable delicacy.

Juan is, typically, passive throughout the poem and 'feminine in feature' (VIII, 52). His appearance in drag before the bossy Sultana almost suggests that he has exchanged gender roles with her. He refuses to carry out this role, however. On his return to the harem, 'ogling' all the girls as he does so, he becomes the covert desire of all the harem who, somehow, sense his obtrusive male presence despite his garb. In this way we have a sense of Nature reasserting her customary patterns in the face of human devices to divert or thwart them. Dudù's dream, in which a bee flies out from an apple she is about to bite and stings her, is a blatant and hilarious device for signalling Juan's love-making to the reader, but it is witty and delicate too. We retain confidence in Juan's instincts and in natural forces, even if they take him away from Haidée and involve him in situations where natural pleasures are hard to disentangle from contrived distractions. We will not be able to maintain this confidence very much longer in *Don Juan*.

The Siege (Cantos VII–VIII)

The narrative structure of the poem prepares us for the disillusion that both the reader and Juan now have to face. Previous episodes have been regularly punctuated by sea journeys, which suggest forgetfulness, recuperation and the irresistible force of natural energies. Now, however, we move immediately from the Turkish seraglio to an account of warfare without any intervening session at sea. No attempt is made to describe Juan and Johnson's escape from Constantinople. In this cutting from one scene to another immediately after Juan's night with Dudù, we again see how unlike a nineteenth-century novel *Don Juan* is.

When, for instance, the hero of Stendhal's famous novel *La Chartreuse de Parme* (1839) blunders on to the field of Waterloo, we are given a strong sense of what it is like to be an outsider caught up in the confusion, butchery and ungraspable scale of modern warfare. This is one of Byron's purposes in the Siege cantos. But Byron also wants to suggest certain definite attitudes to war while, at the same time, forcing us to re-examine our confidence in Juan who, unlike Stendhal's Fabrizio, is a willing participant in the battle.

Byron's conscious attitude to war is straightforward and sensible. When battle is in 'Defence of freedom, country, or of laws', then warfare is legitimate (VII, 40–41; VIII, 4–5). Otherwise 'War's a brain-spattering, windpipe-slitting art' (IX, 4) that is hypocritically disguised by the language of military strategy, glory and honour. Byron had not shared his compatriots' jubilation at English victory in the Battle of Waterloo seven years earlier, but he was prepared to fight in the Greek War of Independence and there drilled 'in proper person' Greek troops, just as Suvarrow, the Russian general, does (VII, 52). There is clear condemnation, therefore, of the Russian soldiers who attack Ismail despite Byron's evident admiration for the style of Suvarrow himself.

In the twentieth century we are so used to anti-war poems and poets that we forget the innumerable celebrations of battle, courage and codes of honour that are the norm in most literary traditions. Cantos VII and VIII recall Homer's battles and formulas in order to mock and attack this tradition. Canto VII describes the preparation for the attack on Ismail and Canto VIII describes the battle itself, but there is no real shape to these cantos because warfare here is chaotic and murderously haphazard rather than gloriously defined. 'Stray troops', for instance, 'wandered up and down as in a dream' (VIII, 72). In Canto VIII, however, there are three focal points that stand out from 'the infinities of agony' (VIII, 13).

Seven stanzas of digression on Daniel Boone (VIII, 61–7) make up the first of these. Byron had read about Boone, an American who deliberately lived away from civilization in the woods of Kentucky. Boone brought up numerous children and remained healthy and active into old age. He is thus in poignant and damning contrast to the soldiers who participate in one of 'thy great joys, civilization' (VIII, 68). Unlike Boone, independent and procreative, they are under orders to cover the field of battle's 'ghastly wilderness' with young corpses (VIII, 112). Boone, as 'the child/Of Nature', stands in the usual opposition to 'large society' (VIII, 68). However, just as in the shipwreck section, there is a worrying kinship here between destruction and Nature. In the last desperate skirmish of the attack, 'War forgot his own destructive art/In more destroying Nature' (VIII, 82).

The rescue of Leila, a little Turkish girl (VIII, 90–102), provides a contrast of a different kind. Leila is 'A female child of ten years' who tries to hide in a heap of bodies 'lulled in bloody rest'. Cossacks are about to kill her, but Juan intervenes and saves her. The image of the innocent girl with 'large eyes' and 'A pure, transparent, pale, yet radiant face' suggests defencelessness, innocence and spiritual strength in the midst of battle horrors. Juan's rescue of her associates him momentarily with an innocence that he and the poem seem to have lost.

Finally, in the moving stanzas on the death of the Tartar khan and his five sons (VIII, 104–19), Byron pays tribute to the very Homeric stereotypes of high style in death which, elsewhere, he pillories.

These three sections and the balanced account of Suvarrow's generalship counter the flippant and bitter tone of Byron's version of war here, but that tone prevails none the less. The warfare is between soldiers of the Sultan, whom we met in Canto V, and Catherine the Great of Russia, whom we will meet in Canto IX. It is, therefore, caused by power politics and 'the world's masters' (IX, 4), though we cannot smugly leave the blame there. When we are shown Juan and Johnson trampling over dead bodies,

> Firing and thrusting, slashing, sweating, glowing
> But fighting thoughtlessly enough . . .
>
> (VIII, 19)

we must be alarmed by the way in which Juan's natural spirits seem to make him fully at home on the battlefield. 'Glowing', for instance, a word used here of battle energies, is associated throughout the poem, as we have seen, with the apparently different intensities of erotic passion. The three sections that we have shown to stand out from the carnage of battle celebrate innocence and the love of parents for children, not erotic love. On the contrary the old Tartar khan's eldest son fights and dies with a specific fusion of sexual and aggressive passion (VIII, 111–15). The poem does not allow us, then, to fall into such simplifications as 'make love not war', for the underlying energies of both may be indistinguishable rather than opposed. Usually in *Don Juan* the insistence upon such unmentionable connections is a matter for comic mirth, but we cannot laugh much at this connection, for it undermines our whole confidence in Don Juan himself and in the natural instincts that he embodies. If we have not understood this important point clearly enough, the next section of the poem proceeds to rub our noses in it.

Catherine the Great (Cantos IX–X)

In many ways this is the least memorable narrative section in *Don Juan*. Byron had not visited Russia, unlike almost all the other places mentioned in the poem, and there is a want of corroborating detail. Yet it is a real pivot in the poem and is crucial to our proper understanding of it.

So far, in every section of the poem we have tried to indicate Byron's invariable habit of qualifying the values that he nevertheless proposes to us. Haidée is marvellous, but there are things wrong with her and with her love for Juan. So it is always in Byron's world. But Catherine the Great is what she immediately appears to be, neither more nor less. Catherine was Empress of Russia, an astute but ruthless woman who was notorious for her sexual appetites. She thus connects together sex and war, domination and femininity, life and death, in the most explicit way. Where, for instance, Haidée brings Juan back to life after his near-death in the sea, Catherine puts him to work immediately as her lover after his immersion in the bloody warfare that she has herself ordained. Instead of the mimic death and renewal in the sea that has punctuated Juan's previous adventures, Catherine is herself a 'sea of life's dry land' (IX, 56). It is best to let Byron make the point for us. He could not do so more plainly. The quotation in the first line quoted below is from Horace ('the most dreadful cause of all wars'), the addressee throughout is the sexual organs of women, and the consequent sexual puns here and throughout this section are supposed to be blatant and unfunny ('falls and rises', 'at a stand'):

> Oh thou *teterrima causa* of all *belli* –
>   Thou gate of life and death – thou nondescript!
> Whence is our exit and our entrance. Well I
>   May pause in pondering how all souls are dipt
> In thy perennial fountain. How men fell, I
>   Know not since knowledge saw her branches stript
> Of her first fruit; but how he falls and rises
> Since, thou has settled beyond all surmises.
>
> Some call thee 'the worst cause of war', but I
>   Maintain thou art the best, for after all
> From thee we come, to thee we go, and why
>   To get at thee not batter down a wall
> Or waste a world, since no one can deny
>   Thou dost replenish worlds both great and small?
> With or without thee all things at a stand
> Are or would be, thou sea of life's dry land!
>
> Catherine, who was the grand epitome
>   Of that great cause of war or peace or what
> You please (it causes all the things which be,
>   So you may take your choice of this or that) –
> Catherine, I say, was very glad to see
> The handsome herald . . .

(IX, 55–7)

To be as clear as this about life's indifference to death because of the indefinite capacity for replenishment built into the dynamics of existence removes all the glamour of sexual attraction. We can no longer trust Nature or Juan. Indeed, they now seem to be in league with the mass destruction of the Siege of Ismail. We can no longer react with enthusiasm, therefore, for Juan's escape from death and renewed sexual life. Of course Byron is satirizing Catherine's Court and European power politics, but he seems to have lost confidence in any positive energies that remain untainted by the corruptions of life.

It comes as no surprise, then, that Juan falls ill and his condition 'augured of the dead' (X, 39). He is unable to sustain his role as lover. Sexual love disappears from the poem altogether for the time being, because we have lost confidence in its value. As we look back on the poem, we begin to fear that the entire sequence of Juan's love-encounters until now has been marked out for this destination from the beginning. Catherine seems to be not just another woman in Juan's history, but an emblem of Woman and Sexual Life, one that includes and reduces every love-episode to a single formula.

Don Juan markedly alters character at this point and any reading of it must account for this change and decide whether we should now stress the poem's collapse into nihilism and incoherence or look for a different kind of unity in it.

The Narrator's Cantos (Cantos X–XII)

To assist Juan's recovery of health, Catherine reluctantly allows him to leave Russia and sends him on a diplomatic mission to England, where he is to stay for the rest of the poem. We could therefore take the last seven cantos of *Don Juan* together as the 'English' cantos, but it is more helpful to take Cantos XIII–XVII, set in Norman Abbey, separately. The reason for this is that the Norman Abbey cantos take shape as a section and again interest us by their developing story, whereas Cantos X–XII are entirely dominated by the narrator, who seems to plan and control them from the outside. We can understand why this is so if we think back to Catherine the Great and the Siege. The first half of *Don Juan*, however complex its adjustments, depends upon a simple confidence in love, Nature and the happy effects of chance. Juan will always survive to encounter yet another glowing female face. He leaves behind him, it is true, a trail of dead, immured or stricken women, wounded husbands, dead fathers and drowned sailors, but Byron is always able to manipulate or bludgeon us into carrying on with some enthusiasm for life and for his poem. Taken together, Catherine the Great and the Siege put a stop to this and prevent us from looking to unexpected narrative incidents, the always renewed imperative of loving or to Juan himself for the moment. Only the narrator, the other energy in the poem, is still left intact and he has to keep the show going by himself.

The only narrative incident of any note in this section is Juan's meeting with four footpads who try to mug him in Canto XI (10–20), but this anecdote is put in to satirize England's reputation as a law-abiding country rather than to engage Juan in new adventures. Everything that happens in these cantos is generalized. The ways of England's upper-class society, their sexual hypocrisy and the daily routines of pointless, empty lives are Byron's object of attention here, not Juan. The timetable of Juan's English life is itself sketched out for us (XI, 65–7) as though England has destroyed or subdued the intensity and unpredictability that have hitherto characterized his existence. At the end of Canto XII, however, we are told that something 'Occurred' to Juan (XII, 85): a new love-affair, which will now engage the poem.

Norman Abbey (Cantos XIII–XVII)

When, in the second stanza of Canto XIII, we are introduced immediately to 'The Lady Adeline Amundeville', it seems likely that she will be the occasion of the occurrence promised at the end of Canto XII. As her character is gradually set out for us, and she is described in greater detail than anyone else in the poem, she seems to epitomize the coldness, decorum and suppressed passions of English high society.

Although Adeline does lie at the centre of Cantos XIII and XIV, and 'in her way too was a heroine' (XIV, 90), she is unexpectedly displaced in the final two cantos of the poem. She remains a central object of attention even there, but two other women, Aurora Raby and the Duchess of Fitz-Fulke, take the poem in a new direction altogether while, miraculously, restoring Don Juan's long-lost confidence in life and love. This movement is, perhaps, the most remarkable one in *Don Juan* and, even though the narrative is suddenly interrupted by Byron's decision to go to Greece and by his death there, we can establish the main lines of the very complex pattern that he has set up.

The first thing we notice is the maintenance of the satirical perspective on English life begun in Canto X. This is generalized, dry, compressed, urbane and disenchanted. The narrator's observations have some of the poise of Pope's satires, while reminding us too of Dickens's bitter indignation at English hypocrisy and class coldness in *Bleak House*. Byron's Norman Abbey is situated roughly between Pope's Timon's Villa and Dickens's Chesney Wold in date and in mode.

Byron attacks the extravagant deployment of wealth in order to keep up with fashion or impress others. Hence he ridicules the French meals of Norman Abbey and elaborate plans for redesigning the ancient house in the latest mock-Gothic style. He attacks the political corruption involved in buying votes and maintaining sinecures, and the larger corruptions of justice such disguised self-interest serves. These are familiar targets of satire but Byron's dislike of English ways assumes considerable proportions. It includes not only the stifling inanities of

Tory country house life, with its boorish fox-hunters and vulgar snobbery, but it seems to cover as well the Whig social and intellectual circle that Byron had himself been part of. Almost every aspect of English social life, formal and informal, seems to be pointless, without resonance and without fun.

There are four particular reference points for this onslaught: Lord Henry Amundeville, Lady Adeline and two dinners held on successive nights in Cantos XV and XVI. Lord Henry and Lady Adeline dominate and embody distinctively masculine and feminine spheres of English social life. Lord Henry, a masterly character-sketch again, is continuously active on important matters 'in the councils of the nation' (XIII, 14) and in local affairs. He is 'Cool and quite English, imperturbable' (XIII, 14). Where, in other cantos, Byron satirizes Russian or Turkish politics through the figure of the monarch, here he castigates the dominance of a powerful landed class who throughout the eighteenth century had virtually ruled England in their own interest. Lord Henry is a patron, diplomat, a justice of the peace and a landowner who raises money by mortgaging part of his estate. He presides over county social life and, through his influence, fixes local elections, but he also deals out justice to unmarried mothers and awards prizes for champion pigs and ploughmen (XVI, 60–61).

Lady Adeline supports all her husband's endeavours. She is beautiful, intelligent, artistic and well-read (XVI, 47). She is endowed with consummate social poise. She presides over the inner arrangements of the house that are her own sphere of influence and she gains there by calculation and charm the power that her husband seeks directly in public life. They are a formidable pair whom Byron satirizes but does not burlesque or ridicule. Their marriage epitomizes the preferred form of English relationships: 'Serene and noble, conjugal, but cold' (XIV, 86).

The first of the two dinner parties (at the end of Canto XV) is for the house guests alone and is simply a satire on pretentious and extravagant eating habits. The second, in Canto XVI, is open to anyone of importance in the local community as well and here Byron is more concerned with the guests than with the food. Here too we see Lady Adeline at work 'watching, witching, condescending / To the consumers of fish, fowl and game' (XVI, 95) in order to maintain the Amundevilles' social and political influence through their support. She plays 'her grand role' splendidly, betraying herself only occasionally by a look 'Of weariness or scorn' (XVI, 96).

These meals are empty and joyless yet they are keenly looked forward to (XIII, 102) by guests who find it hard to fill their day with other activities. They epitomize the spiritual blight of England, high society and modern life. These dinner parties form the climax, then, of the satire on England that began in Canto X, but, having accustomed us to think in one way, Byron now asks us to think in another way altogether. Juan himself is no longer caught up in this form of life or in the two dinners that express it. The Duchess of Fitz-Fulke, the ghost of the Black Friar and Aurora Raby are responsible for this change. Roughly speaking, Aurora and the ghost represent the spiritual resonances and resources that modern English society lacks and the Duchess embodies the fun that it somehow misses too.

Aurora is the most important of these. She is a beautiful orphan who is a temporary guest at the house. She, not Adeline, turns out to be the real heroine of the final cantos to whom Juan is instinctively drawn. She is a heroine on such a scale that she can recall and, in some ways, surpass Haidée (XV, 58). She belongs thus to the story of the poem that she reinvigorates, though she is so profoundly thoughtful (XVI, 48) that she appears to know far more than the narrator does. Hence she is a lynchpin capable of binding narrator and narrative together as no one else in the poem can. In addition she represents a realized ideal that we can set against the arid bustle of Norman Abbey's daytime life. Although the narrator can bitterly set out the charges against this life, he is himself so close to it that he cannot offer anything superior.

Aurora tells us a great deal about the kind of poem *Don Juan* is, so she will be discussed again in the pages on comedy (pp. 122–33). How does she fit into the final cantos? If we collect together all Byron's references to her (principally XV, 43–58, 77–85; XVI, 92–4, 106–8), we see that she has the apparently untainted innocence of Haidée while also knowing all about the Fall:

> She looked as if she sat by Eden's door
> And grieved for those who could return no more
> (XV, 45)

Hence she is, in a marvellous phrase, both 'Radiant and grave'. She remains innocent but fully understands the character of experience. This makes her a crucial figure at the end of a poem that seems to have lost touch with innocence and associates understanding with bitterness. If therefore Aurora is, although as lovely as Haidée, less 'warm' than her (XV, 58), nevertheless she cannot end up as Haidée, does, entombed in a ruined 'Paradise' (IV, 72). Instead of this, Aurora seems to draw sustenance from the ruins of the ancient abbey house. It is what Aurora is in touch with that counts. Adeline has, like any heroine in a nineteenth-century novel, a fully formed exterior and interior, yet Juan doubts 'how much of Adeline was real' (XVI, 96). For Adeline is in touch with nothing at all.

When Juan is placed between Aurora and Adeline at the first dinner party, he is drawn to Aurora's silence and her mysterious, substantial presence, whereas Adeline, though complex and active, is wholly unsubstantial. More than a character contrast is at stake here. Byron dramatizes this for us by a deft and telling fable of ownership. Who, he asks, is the rightful owner of Norman Abbey?

Norman Abbey is a typical country house with typical guests, but it has a name and distinct life of its own. Lord Henry's London house is 'in Blank Blank square' (XIII, 25) because Byron's satire at this point is generalized and not linked to any particular fictional action. In Norman Abbey, however, character and action again begin to take on an independent life, as they did in the first half of the poem. The house itself is brilliantly described (XIII, 55–72) before we have any account of its inhabitants. It is part of 'a happy valley' beside 'a lucid lake'. It seems to be in intimate contact with the surrounding landscape and this seems accentuated by the ruined remains of the abbey church that stood there before the Reformation. A statue of 'The Virgin-Mother' still stands above the great, empty, west window and the monks' abandoned quire still sounds with eerie music:

> But in the noontide of the moon and when
>   The wind is wingèd from one point of heaven,
> There moans a strange unearthly sound, which then
>   Is musical, a dying accent driven
> Through the huge arch, which soars and sinks again.
>
> (XIII, 63)

Norman Abbey seems to be two houses therefore. The Amundevilles own and live in one of these. But the house has another secret life of its own. It seems, especially at night, to participate in the life of Nature, it remains loyal to its own forgotten history, and it seems to be mysteriously connected to the space that surrounds it.

Aurora is connected directly to this other life of the house. She is a Catholic, 'And deemed that fallen worship far more dear / Perhaps because 'twas fallen' (XV, 46). Though an orphan she remains consciously loyal, unlike Haidée, to the inheritance of her fathers. Hence she represents in the new secular Norman Abbey the force and claims of the 'old faith and feelings' that built and shaped the original abbey. Like the statue of the Virgin-Mother, with whom she is paralleled,

> There was awe in the homage which she drew;
>   Her spirit seemed as seated on a throne
> Apart from the surrounding world and strong
> In its own strength, most strange in one so young.
>   (XV, 47)

In Aurora too there is the same mysterious sense of intimate kinship with space that the house has:

> The worlds beyond this world's perplexing waste
>   Had more of her existence, for in her
> There was a depth of feeling to embrace
> Thoughts, boundless, deep, but silent too as space.
>   (XVI, 48)

To place such a character as this alongside Adeline and make her emerge out of what appears to be the unshakeable grip of satire in the last cantos is, I think, the most surprising and the finest thing in English Romantic poetry. She reactivates that sense of freedom and Nature that has been so important in the poem, but Nature, civilization, and art seem now to be reconciled in the sweet austerity of her being. When Juan is drawn to her, he is necessarily drawn away from the daytime social world of the secularized house and its apparent owners to the hidden, enduring resonances of the older house. This is pictured for us by the other great triumph of the last cantos: the story of the Black Friar.

In each of the nights following the two dinners Juan encounters a ghost. In the day between these occurrences, which Juan passes in a daze, Lady Adeline sings a ballad that explains who the ghost is reputed to be. The ghost, it appears, is of a monk who remained in the abbey after its dissolution by Henry VIII and refuses to accept the new owners' rights to the house. Hence

> *But beware! beware of the Black Friar!*
> *He still retains his sway,*
> *For he is yet the church's heir*
> *Whoever may be the lay.*

> *Amundeville is lord by day,*
> *But the monk is lord by night.*
> (XVI, between 40–41)

On the first occasion when Juan meets this ghost (XVI, 20–25), it is, though told with wit, an experience of pure terror that shocks him into silence throughout the following day and this associates him with the natural silence of Aurora (XVI, 105–7). On the second occasion (XVI, 113–23) the ghost appears to have the same effect; however, when pursued, it turns out to be not 'stony death' but 'something much like flesh and blood'. The Duchess of Fitz-Fulke has in fact used the legend of the ghost as a disguise, both as a prank and in order to gain Juan's bedroom. It is a mistake to assume that the first ghost is also the young Duchess in disguise, as we are bound, momentarily, to imagine. The behaviour of the two 'ghosts' is quite distinct and we find the Duchess asking for 'a still more detailed narration / Of this same mystic Friar's curious doings' (XVI, 53) after the first haunting. She must do so in order to consolidate a plan that has suddenly formed in her mind when she hears the story and finds out the connection it has with Juan.

The connections established by these ghost narratives bewilder us by their contrariety. Farce and terror, sex and religion, life, death, space, night, practical jokes, Gothic fact and Gothic parody – all merge in the two ghost stories and their connection with the opposed figures of Aurora Raby and Fitz-Fulke. Through them the spiritual resonance and heedless fun carefully kept out of the Amundevilles' correct English life come bursting back into the poem.

What would have happened next in the poem if Byron had been able to extend it we do not know and cannot reliably guess. It seems clear that, in Byron's original scheme, Adeline would have been divorced by Lord Henry on the grounds of adultery with Juan and that the ghost's appearance heralds this coming misfortune in the future of the usurping owners of the abbey. How this would have fitted in with Fitz-Fulke's 'dead set' at Juan and Juan's movement towards the incomparable Aurora is hard to imagine. The next canto, which stops abruptly after fourteen stanzas, begins 'The world is full of orphans' and so, we must assume, would have been about Aurora. It is appropriate, needless to say, that the poem should end suddenly through Byron's death at a point where narrative confidence has been recovered and we are left eagerly anticipating further events that we cannot easily predict. After all, we could not have predicted, at the outset of Canto XIII, the creation of Aurora Raby or the remarkable authority of Byron's inventiveness in the last complete canto of *Don Juan*.

Digressions and the Narrator

We have described the general character of the narrator, the double focus of the poem and the importance of digressions in the section on Sources, Influences and Themes. When we first pick up *Don Juan*, it seems as if the digressions are its life and soul, that they are as impromptu and haphazard as they claim to be, and that they are written directly by the author in his own voice. Let us look at a characteristic digressive passage from the end of Canto III and try to assess its function and effect.

We can begin at stanza 78, which introduces us to the poet present at Haidée's banquet, leads into his 'The Isles of Greece' and then into a digression proper that lasts virtually until the end of the canto.

The Greek poet and his song belong to the story of Haidée's isle, but the character-sketch of the poet is used by Byron to pillory his own contemporaries, Wordsworth and Southey, rather than to further the narrative. Hence the first group of stanzas is both digressive and narrative in form. This is quite normal in the poem. It is not always easy to decide whether the poet is digressing or not. This is especially so in the English cantos. The transition to digression proper is sometimes by imperceptible stages, sometimes by abrupt transition. On some occasions it is accomplished simply by a shift of attention so that we are asked to notice something that cannot obtain within the narrative. At other times our eyes remains on the narrative, but the narrator's tone is so intrusive that this may become our primary object of attention.

In the previous section of Canto III we have had an extensive description of Juan and Haidée's banquet. The narrator has reminded us of his presence throughout by little interjections such as these:

> Cloves, cinnamon, and saffron too were boiled
> Up with the coffee, which (I think) they spoiled.
> (III, 70)

> Of all the dresses I select Haidée's.
> (III, 70)

Nevertheless the narrator's eyes and ours have been on what he is describing. When he comes to the Greek poet, however, the narrator's own thoughts begin to dominate his observation to such an extent that

107

his description itself begins to seem like a digression from which we ought to be summoned back to the story:

> But he had genius; when a turncoat has it
>   The *vates irritabilis* takes care
> That without notice few full moons shall pass it.
>   Even good men like to make the public stare.
> But to my subject – let me see – what was it?
>   Oh – the third canto and the pretty pair,
>
> (III, 81)

Here the keyword 'turncoat' alerts us at once to Byron's own distaste for Wordsworth's, Coleridge's and Southey's abandonment of their former liberal principles and 'the public'; that is, the contemporary audience and social world is more in the narrator's mind than his fictional Greek poet. Hence the narrator treats this like a digression and ostentatiously casts his mind back to the story.

After 'The Isles of Greece' the narrator launches into an extensive digression in a sustained voice of his own. Attempts to return to the narrative such as these:

> But let me to my story. I must own,
>   If I have any fault, it is digression,
>
> (III, 96)

are swamped by renewed digressions in a manner that we have come to expect in *Don Juan*. At one point the narrator does manage to write a whole stanza of narrative (101), but this immediately initiates a new pattern of digression.

In digressive passages as lengthy as these, distinct lines of thought are usually generated. The twenty-four stanzas that follow 'The Isles of Greece' can be divided into three sections with a two-stanza tail-piece. The first four stanzas (87–90) modulate naturally away from the Greek poet and his song into a discussion of the way in which written words outlast both those who write and those who are written about. The tone is wry, expertly keeping at bay both an elegiac and a bitter note that threaten to take over. The narrator often maintains his poise exactly at this level:

> ... To what straits old Time reduces
> Frail man, when paper, even a rag like this,
> Survives himself, his tomb, and all that's his.
>
> (III, 88)

From considering the greater durability of a written biography than an actual life, the narrator shifts easily into an account of famous lives, especially lives of poets, that he has read; this in turn brings him to the lives of contemporary poets and hence to a familiar attack upon Wordsworth, Coleridge and Southey. These are criticized first for their bad lives (as political turncoats) and then for their bad verse (in comparison with Pope and Dryden). This takes us up to stanza 100 and reads like a separate section. We are no longer on a Greek island, but, on the other hand, the discussion of poetry and its relationship to the life of the poet has grown naturally out of the character-sketch of the Greek poet within the narrative.

In stanza 101 the story is momentarily revived and we see Juan and Haidée admiring the sunset together. In the next stanza, however, the narrator sets off on an extensive tribute to evening of his own that takes up the next seven stanzas and nearly completes the canto. Again, the digression is set in motion by circumstances within the narrative, but to be redirected back to digression after so perfunctory a reminder of the story makes digression seem the norm. It does accomplish one narrative effect nevertheless, even when not appearing to do so. The story we momentarily pick up again has advanced a little in time, as though it had been going on by itself while the narrator is digressing. Sometimes after a digression we are restored to exactly the same point that we had earlier left, but Byron often takes advantage of this way of suggesting the passing of time as he does here.

In the first part of the digression we saw how Byron maintained a particular tone of voice; now we find a rich deployment of different voices, so that the narrator can actually interrupt his own digression much as he interrupts the narrative. Look, for instance, at the opening of these three successive stanzas:

> Ave Maria! 'Tis the hour of prayer!
> Ave Maria! 'Tis the hour of love!
> Ave Maria! May our spirits dare
> Look up to thine and to thy Son's above!
> (103)

> Some kinder casuists are pleased to say
> In the nameless print that I have no devotion;
> But set those persons down with me to pray,
> And you shall see who has the properest notion
> (104)

109

> Sweet hour of twilight! In the solitude
> Of the pine forest and the silent shore
> Which bounds Ravenna's immemorial wood.
>
> (105)

Here an apostrophe to Our Lady, both stylized as a formulaic prayer ('Ave Maria! Ave Maria! Ave Maria!') and unmistakably Byron's ('May our spirits dare'), is interrupted by the tone of a reasonable man talking to himself in a way intended to be overheard ('Some kinder casuists', 'those persons', 'you shall see'). This in turn is interrupted by a direct apostrophe to evening ('Sweet hour of twilight . . . How have I loved the twilight hour and thee!'). Byron is present in these lines when he is complaining about contemporary criticism of his absence of 'devotion', in his evocation of the devotion and in the sense of his intense pleasure in the Italian landscape that surrounds him in his place of writing. But Byron's presence is not the straightforward thing it was earlier. Byron's verse seems to gain energy here from the appropriation of other voices than his own. We are surprised to find his voice so emphatically within the hymn to Our Lady, even if he suddenly seems to step back as though embarrassed by what others might say about this. He seems to claim more and less devotion than his English readers would accept. Similarly, his evocation of 'Ravenna's immemorial wood' is a tribute to what Boccaccio and Dryden have made him feel about it. Dryden's tale 'Theodore and Honoria', a favourite of Byron's, is based on a Boccaccio story and set in the 'evergreen forest' which hence is made 'haunted ground to me'. It should come as no surprise that the next two stanzas (107, 108), still in praise of evening, are loose translations of Sappho and of Dante, though given as the narrator's own. Evening is thus the occasion for a display of invention, learning and feeling that begins and ends with the tolling of the vesper-bell (102, 108). Byron is doing all this and yet the success of it depends upon allowing other voices to speak through him. The exalted sentiment, and a confidence in gentleness that seems to fuse Nature, erotic love and religious feeling, flow finally into a surprising little anecdote about Nero (109) whose tomb was strewn with flowers by 'Some hands unseen'. The point is that even a 'wretch' and a 'destroyer' like Nero have felt and caused kindness, if this story is credited. But at this furthest reach of sentiment, the narrator engineers our recoil:

> But I'm digressing. What on earth has Nero
> Or any such like sovereign buffoons
> To do with the transactions of my hero,
>
> (III, 110)

and the canto is brought to its conclusion.

Not all digressions in *Don Juan* are exactly like this, but we can now make a number of general comments that apply to it and many of the others.

Self-consciousness, the state and nature of poetry and politics, bitter and elegiac reflections upon death and time held just in check, tender apostrophes to beauty and to human feelings – these often interrupt narrative in *Don Juan*, though, as here, they echo and parallel its concerns. We frequently attribute all of these to a superintending personality whom we think of as Byron. It is Byron, after all, who has read Dryden and Boccaccio in stanzas 105–6 and it is he who has seen 'Ravenna's immemorial wood'. Yet it cannot be Byron all the time. Often, it is true, this personality maintains a cool and recognizable temper (III, 87–100), though at other times he modulates rapidly through an array of voices that he does not himself originate but is momentarily identical with.

Many readers of Byron's poetry and of his incomparable letters become confused as to where Byron really is. He seems to change from one thing into another without warning. He appears to give himself away completely and yet remain in hiding. It is a mistake to locate 'Byron' within the poem. If he is the narrator, who writes the rest of the poem? Who decides the balance between digression and narration? If he writes down what is 'uppermost' with him, why does it always come out in complex and exact stanzas? Nevertheless it is also a mistake to explain away the peculiar directness and immediacy of the poem or to imagine that we can dispense with its author altogether. We can illustrate the impossibility of doing either of these things by a detail at the second dinner party in Norman Abbey. Here the narrator claims that

> I sate next that o'erwhelming son of heaven,
> The very powerful Parson Peter Pith,
> The loudest wit I e'er was deafened with.
>
> I knew him in his livelier London days,
> (XVI, 81–2)

Only the narrator, not Byron, could sit at a fictional table in Norman Abbey set at a period of time when Byron was not quite, or was only just, born. On the other hand only Byron, not the narrator, had actually known the real parson Sydney Smith who is transparently referred to here.

Any person has a history and a recognizable range of voice. Lord

111

Byron is one such. We encounter in *Don Juan* something of Byron's history, experience, ideas and feelings. We catch tones of voice that others who knew him would recognize as no one else's but his. But we become a person through mingling with and imitating the styles of thought and feeling of others whom we have met in life or through art. Moreover, however much our lives are shaped through public encounters, inherited traditions and private histories, we remain open to a future that we cannot control or predict – until we die that is. All this is obvious enough, but we forget it. Byron never did so. His sense of humour, his religious sense and his common sense kept him in touch with these basic truths. Political commentators, diarists, psychologists and most novelists select intelligible patterns out of the bewildering interactions that form our lives. Byron, unlike these, wishes to stay as close as possible to the interactions themselves and thus offers us, as he repeatedly insists, an imitation, or mimesis, of 'things existent'.

The business of shaping a coherent personality for ourselves out of our past history and of co-operating with future, unpredictable events as they unfold is 'life', but it is also very similar to the art of *Don Juan*. Byron there reshapes inherited patterns and genres while making a display of his co-operation with unplanned incidents and his delighted dependence upon outlandish words provoked by rhyme and metre. Hence the narrator's interruption of the narrative will take us away from the invented world of fiction (Juan's adventures) and remind us of a real man and a real world outside the text. In another way, however, the narrator's interruptions will remind us of the parallels between fiction and reality. If, for instance, the narrator seems to have a stable and recognizable personality, as in the first part of the digression we examined, this will only be because it is regulated in much the same way as the author regulates the life of a fictional character. On the other hand, where we seem to lose the narrator in a succession of voices, some of them borrowed from others, fictionality here will be putting us in touch with the truth that all persons try out voices for size and maintain their self only in finding and losing their many selves. So the less sense we have of the narrator as a distinct and predictable personality, the more closely we know him.

As *Don Juan* proceeds, we are drawn deeper into this puzzle or, as the narrator calls it, this 'abyss' or 'labyrinth'. It is, currently, a very fashionable puzzle to be drawn into. Much recent criticism of literature has claimed that all life is a supreme fiction. According to this view, we make up everything – God, science, history, politics and the self – in more or less the same way as we make up stories. When we read stories, however, we are now told that we contemplate (or modern readers should do) our own talent for making patterns that can be interpreted over and over again rather than being taken in by any of the patterns themselves as being 'real'. This is what literature is and it is a mistake to refer it to anything outside itself. This view, now current in the West and argued with considerable sophistication, is not so very far away from the classroom dictum that a poem is different for every person that reads it. Many critics have argued or assumed that *Don Juan* is an instance of this modern assurance, but it should be quite clear that it is not.

It is helpful here to remind ourselves again that *Don Juan* was written when Romantic poetry, with its tendency to exalt human imagination over everything else, was forming dominant taste and received vocabulary as, by and large, it still does. Byron's dislike of Wordsworth, Southey, Coleridge and the new poetics is written into *Don Juan*. But we should not see his poem as simply providing a rearguard action in defence of the older views ('Thou shalt believe in Milton, Dryden, Pope'). Many Romantic writers, though caught-up in the new claims for imagination, could see the difficulties and even absurdities of some of them. Some Romantic poems dramatize the failure of the imagination to deliver a new world or regenerate an old one. Others, especially on the Continent, adopted a pose of 'Romantic irony' that enabled them to remain disenchantedly in touch with the enchanted places of their imagining. Byron's great poem, with its abundantly imagined locations and detached narrator, clearly forms part of these patterns of his time, but it is not to be neatly packaged away as simply an instance of them.

What interests Byron most in *Don Juan* is the nature of 'the given'. He can make up characters, events and a world, and does do, but he always wants to let us know that he is doing this. He wants also to share with us the puzzle and the mystery of where the world of his own making and the larger world not of his own making come from. The torrent of Romantic creativity tends to be self-referring. It sometimes seems so with the narrator of *Don Juan*.

> But Adeline was indifferent, for –
>   Now for a commonplace – beneath the snow,
> As a volcano holds the lava more
>   Within, et cetera. Shall I go on? No.
> I hate to hunt down a tired metaphor,
>   (XIII, 36)

113

Volcanoes, it would seem from these lines, have less energy than the mind that can summon or reject them for its own purposes. Whenever such ideas as these are turned into a theory, however, the narrator rejects it with scorn, as in this characteristic and splendid outburst beginning Canto XI:

> When Bishop Berkeley said there was no matter
>   And proved it, 'twas no matter what he said.
> They say his system 'tis in vain to batter,
>   Too subtle for the airiest human head;
> And yet who can believe it! . . .
>
> What a sublime discovery 'twas to make the
>   Universe universal egotism!
> That's all ideal – *all* ourselves. I'll stake the
>   World (be it what you will) that that's no schism . . .
>
> And that which after all my spirit vexes
> Is that I can find no spot where man can rest eye on
>   Without confusion of the sorts and sexes,
> Of being, stars, and this unriddled wonder,
> The world, which at the worst's a glorious blunder,
>
> If it be chance, or if it be according
>   To the old Text, still better . . .
>
> And therefore will I leave off metaphysical
>   Discussion, which is neither here nor there.
> If I agree that what is, is; then this I call
>   Being quite perspicuous and extremely fair.
>
> (XI, 1–5)

Byron's attachment to 'what is' is the foundation of the poem. The device of the narrator reminds us, like the placards supposed to be held up by actors in some of Brecht's plays, that we should not allow ourselves to be wholly caught up in Byron's poem, for it is a fiction. On the other hand the narrator also reminds us that we are, all the time, caught up in a real world of chance occurrence and intelligible pattern that seem to operate much like the narrator's poem. The question is, therefore, if the real world holds together by 'chance' or 'according/To the old Text' (i.e. the Bible). In other words, is the world made up of random events or is it held together by a story? And if the latter, is that because human beings cannot help imposing human fictions on what they see or because the world actually is held together by God's mysterious, and only partly discernible, story? We cannot answer these questions comfortably, but we cannot avoid them either. Certainly the last complete canto of *Don Juan* refers to them over and over again.

It is for this reason that, if we continue the digression from Canto XI quoted above, we find the narrator admitting 'I grow much more orthodox' (XI, 5). The reference here, like most of Byron's to religion, is hedged with irony, but should be taken seriously. The emergence of Aurora Raby in Canto XV, an orthodox Christian treated with un-qualified respect, and the device of the two ghost stories in Canto XVI offered to us by the narrator as fictions that are impossible to believe in and yet that must be believed in exactly the same way as religious faith (XVI, 5–7), are an extraordinarily ambitious attempt to run together the competing claims of chance, fiction and faith as explaining devices for 'what is'. That we find ourselves doing this at the end of *Don Juan* is only possible because the narrator and the digressions are not a stable mechanism set apart from the poem but form part of its developing life. Religious underpinning eventually becomes essential to *Don Juan* be-cause it alone will substantiate, authorize and explain the identity of chance, fiction and truth that the poem and its narrator find themselves committed to.

Style

Byron writes *Don Juan, Beppo* and *The Vision of Judgement* in *ottava rima*. Why did he choose this stanza form? We have seen earlier that this verse form had not been much used in English verse, though it had been used in a recent comic poem by John Hookham Frere. In Italy *ottava rima* had been a staple form for centuries.

There were two main reasons for its neglect by English poets. Spen-serian stanzas, which Byron had used in *Childe Harold*, constituted a rival mode which, given Spenser's popularity with poets, was far more familiar to English ears. Secondly, both stanza forms rely upon repeated rhymes, which are very hard to sustain in English. For example, most of the words in my last sentence end in consonants. The one Italian word in the sentence, 'stanza', ends like most Italian words, in a vowel. As there are far fewer vowels than consonants, it is obvious that it is much easier to rhyme in Italian than in English.

Byron sought out this difficulty because he wanted an intricate and obvious verse form to set against the free flow of the poem. Rhyme also connects unlikely pairs of words, concepts and things together. Since such connection forms a major part of *Don Juan*'s purpose and humour, it is easy to see why the sustained feat of rhyming that *Don Juan* demands is wholly appropriate to it.

The stanzas in *Don Juan* rhyme a b a b a b c c. The final couplet, using a new rhyme, gives an effect of closure and is, almost invariably, followed by a full stop. Byron rarely carries the sentence across stanzas, as he frequently does in the later cantos of *Childe Harold*. You will find two examples where he does so in Canto V (18–19) and Canto IV (10–11). This means that, for all Byron's self-conscious escapades with rhyme and diction, his stanzas are written with much greater regularity and decorum than we at first think.

The metre of the poem confirms this. If the lines are read rapidly with the eye, they almost seem to be prose; but if they are heard as they are read, and they always should be, they are almost as regular as lines by Pope or Dryden and far more regular than, say, the blank verse in Shakespeare's *The Tempest*. The penultimate stanza in the poem is a fair example of this:

> I leave the thing a problem, like all things.
>> The morning came, and breakfast, tea and toast,
> Of which most men partake, but no one sings.
>> The company, whose birth, wealth, worth have cost
> My trembling lyre already several strings,
>> Assembled with our hostess and mine host.
> The guests dropped in, the last but one, Her Grace,
> The latest, Juan with his virgin face.

(XVII, 13)

The verse here is deadpan and assured. It may be helpful to indicate both its regularity and its lovely cadence. 'Cost' is not an exact rhyme, though it is an eye-rhyme with 'host'; otherwise all the rhymes are masculine (i.e. coincide with a stressed syllable) and precise. Most rhymes in the poem are like this although, of course, we tend to remember the outrageous polysyllabic ones. This is true of the style in general. We notice extreme features of style, even if they are statistically very infrequent, far more readily than the customary mode itself, which we accept without attention. Yet it is the customary mode that is doing most of the work.

The metre is iambic pentameter, as it is throughout the poem except for the Greek song in Canto III and Lady Adeline's ballad in Canto XVI. Iambic pentameter is the staple metre of Chaucer, Shakespeare,

Spenser, Milton, Dryden, Pope, Wordsworth, Tennyson and most other poets. It is so because it most closely resembles breathing and stress patterns in English (not American) customary speech. For this reason it is often hard for the inexperienced reader to detect that it is verse at all. It would, in fact, be hard to write more regularly iambic lines than:

> x / x / x / x / x /
> The morning came, and breakfast, tea and toast,

or
> x / x / x / x / x /
> The guests dropped in, the last but one, Her Grace,

In each line we have five iambic units (unstressed syllable *x* followed by stressed syllable /) making up ten syllables exactly. Iambic pentameter does not involve hearing five very clear stresses in each line. In the last line, for instance,

> / / / /
> The latest Juan with his virgin face

we hear the four syllables marked much more clearly than the others. This is quite common. The pattern established is an entirely relative one and in this pattern 'with' is clearly stressed rather more than the two syllables either side of it. So we still have five iambic units. Where so strict a norm is established, we automatically adjust less regular patterns to it, as here:

> x / x x x / / / x /
> The company whose birth, wealth, worth have cost

We could scan this differently but, on any view, the last syllable of 'company' and the word 'wealth' are weaker and stronger sounds respectively than the strictest pattern would require. Manifestly these cancel each other out. Byron rarely gives us anything less regular metrically than this in *Don Juan*. If a line has eleven syllables, this is almost invariably because the last line is a feminine one (e.g. 'mellow', 'bellow', 'fellow') or because Byron intends us to contract 'even' to 'e'en' or 'several' to 'sev'ral' as in this stanza. Feminine rhymes are most common in the concluding couplet to each stanza, where they increase the effect of closure.

In the stanza quoted above there is a natural pause at the end of each line, except for lines 4–5. Usually there is more enjambment than this, but too much would destroy the metre and the always noticeable rhyme. Enjambment here hides the only inexact rhyme we noted.

If the metre is extremely regular, the cadence is artfully varied. Look, for instance, at the different placing of verbs in these lines and how their different position modifies the run of voice. Sentences too differ in length and construction. Here there are four. Surprisingly, Byron often lets the stanza and the sentence flow together, as in II, 160. In Canto II, for instance, nearly a quarter of the stanzas are made up of a single sentence. The general balance is exactly the same as in Ariosto and Tasso, the great masters of *ottava rima*.

If we read the stanza through aloud, we should be able to catch its pleasing management of sound and silence that support the music and the meaning of the verse. The first line is an aphorism in itself that connects back to the previous stanza. The next two sentences grow in length, culminating in the verb 'Assembled', which reclaims the sense after the intervening clause. After this the last two lines fall away in an exact parallel to their sense ('dropped in' compared with 'Assembled').

The balance of the stanza is helped by intricate cross-references of sound within it. Some of these are fairly obvious such as:

1 2 3 1 4 2 5 2 4 3
My trembling lyre already several strings

Virtually every sound in this line connects with another, as indicated by the numbers. Alliteration of *l* and *s* is obvious too. But the pattern here passes beyond this line. We could trace 'trembling' back to and beyond 'wealth' in the previous line and forward to 'Assembled' in the next line, which takes us forward again to 'hostess' and then to 'guests', 'last', 'Grace', 'latest' and 'face'. There are many more such sound patterns in this stanza, often made out of words to which we rarely pay much attention ('dropped in', 'but one', 'Juan', 'virgin').

When therefore Byron tells us that describing Norman Abbey and its guests for more than three cantos has cost 'My trembling lyre already several strings', we should note the evident irony of manner but should not doubt that considerable pains and musical sense have, in fact, been expended in apparently plain and casual verse.

Some of these effects are superb. These two lines, for instance

The morning came, and breakfast, tea and toast,
Of which most men partake, but no one sings.

could not be bettered by Pope or anyone else. There is a delicious irony in the acknowledgement of the irretrievably unpoetic character of everyday experience while, at the same time, turning 'breakfast, tea and toast' into a serene and lasting cadence. The word 'song' or 'sings' often seems to generate an eerie poignancy of wit in Byron, as for example in:

> The grass upon my grave will grow as long
> And sigh to midnight winds, but not to song.
> (IV, 99)

and

> . . . Carelessly I sing,
> But Phoebus lends me now and then a string,
> (VIII, 138)

and

> The night (I sing by night, sometimes an owl
> And now and then a nightingale) is dim,
> (XV, 97)

Byron often wants to move us and to enlarge our capacity for attention like this, but he does not want to forego lucidity and intelligibility. *Don Juan* is nothing other than a poem and everything is poetic within it, but Byron does not want us to jettison habits of attention that are customary in other kinds of writing and talk. In this, he is entering very similar territory to that mapped out in Wordsworth's preface to *Lyrical Ballads*. Wordsworth, of course, launched there a very famous attack on poetic diction and defended prose and the language of a man speaking to men as the best model for good verse. Byron took a very different view of these matters and Wordsworth was shocked by *Don Juan*, though, ironically, Byron's poem achieves some of Wordsworth's aims more convincingly than Wordsworth himself. When, for instance, we praise Byron's ability to sing 'breakfast, tea and toast' despite his disclaimer, we are in fact supporting the Wordsworthian insistence that something lowly and familiar can be defamiliarized and elevated by song. The difference is that Byron's method here is ironical and that the social world of this particular breakfast is aristocratic rather than rustic. It is facts like these that make Byron's views on diction so different from Wordsworth's.

When Wordsworth proposes that the best language for poetry should be based, more or less, on that of simple people speaking directly from the heart, attacking also the existing relationship of poetry to polite society and to a special diction, it is hard for us not to be caught up in the generous democracy of his sentiments. But is he right? Certainly if he is right, non-peasant poets will have to forego their two most obvious resources of vocabulary: their own conversational speech and the inherited phrases of poetry.

Byron's *Don Juan* is a deliberate attempt to write a long poem that does the opposite of Wordsworth's recommendation and, instead, openly incorporates the conversational idioms that he knew or used himself together with words and habits of style that had long been customary in English poetry. In particular this meant building on the poetry of Pope and Dryden rather than rejecting it as a model, for Pope and Dryden, more than anyone else, had fashioned the poetic conventions that came down to the Romantics. Byron makes the point forcefully for us in the digressive passage in Canto III that we looked at earlier. The 'he' in the first line is Wordsworth:

> If he must fain sweep o'er the ethereal plain,
>   And Pegasus runs restive in his 'waggon',
> Could he not beg the loan of Charles's Wain?
>   Or pray Medea for a single dragon?
> Or if too classic for his vulgar brain,
>   He feared his neck to venture such a nag on,
> And he must needs mount nearer to the moon,
> Could not the blockhead ask for a balloon?
>
> 'Pedlars' and 'boats' and 'waggons'! Oh ye shades
>   Of Pope and Dryden, are we come to this?
> That trash of such sort not alone evades
>   Contempt, but from the bathos' vast abyss
> Floats scum-like uppermost, and these Jack Cades
>   Of sense and song above your graves may hiss.
> The 'little boatman' and his 'Peter Bell'
> Can sneer at him who drew 'Achitophel'!
>
>   (III, 99–100)

Byron is here making fun of two recently published poems by Wordsworth, 'The Waggoner' and 'Peter Bell' (Shelley ridiculed the latter in his 'Peter Bell the Third'). He is angry because these poems are attempts to displace the taste for Pope and Dryden, whom Wordsworth had attacked in his 'Essay, Supplementary to the Preface' (*Poems 1815*), by verse that does not make good sense and deliberately seeks out low vocabulary and low life. Byron's reaction here seems snobbish and, in a way, it is. But we should notice how Byron's own stanzas use a low vocabulary of their own ('neck', 'nag', 'blockhead', 'balloon', 'scum', 'Jack Cades'), accommodate too a sophisticated style of speech ('restive', 'to venture', 'he must needs', 'evades contempt') and mix in a few acknowledged poeticisms ('fain sweep', 'ethereal plain', 'Pegasus', 'Oh ye shades', 'vast abyss'). The word 'song' again triggers a wonderful line:

> and these Jack Cades
> Of sense and song above your graves may hiss.

It is for the reader to judge whether this deliberate *mélange* of different dictions by Byron really works. If it does so, Wordsworth's theory cannot be right, for it shows that, whatever Wordsworth says, it is possible to produce a telling and natural idiom that reuses poetic phrases, draws on polite conversation and on colloquial speech. Of course in this example a phrase like 'ethereal plain' is edged with evident irony. Usually, though not always, this is how elevated idioms are treated in *Don Juan*. Byron gives the impression both that he knows what he is doing and that the language he uses is larger than he is and commands his loyalty. What outrages him in Wordsworth's practice was that Wordsworth's poems might suddenly dip like this:

> Hush, there is someone on the stir!
> 'Tis Benjamin the Waggoner.
> ('The Waggoner', 22–3)

but then suddenly claim a more earnest or a more sublime vocabulary without, apparently, calculating the likely effects on the reader.

Wordsworth is a great poet, of course, and we should not judge him via 'The Waggoner', but his best poems are not actually written according to his brilliantly persuasive theories. *Don Juan*, on the other hand, is a poetic theory that lives only in its assured and considered practice.

Shelley said that *Don Juan* was 'wholly new', which it is, but Byron shows us in this that it is possible for a 'wholly new' poem to adapt and reassemble an inherited vocabulary and put it to work alongside current speech. In this way Byron preserves the historically derived conventions that enable us to recognize something as poetry rather than something else while, at the same time, preventing poetry from being a wholly special territory that only primitive men or ultra-sensitive modern spirits would tamper with. He was right about the argument but lost the historical point. *Don Juan* could not avert the strange and, on the whole, depressing future history of English poetry in which, as a result of social changes and Romantic theories, poetry became the specialized preserve of smaller and smaller groups of people and the rumour that it once commanded sane and central territories of thought and feeling was itself lost.

Every time we read *Don Juan*, therefore, we should find ourselves involved in an argument about style that we should take seriously. Many familiar twentieth-century assumptions about the history and style of poetry are on the wrong track, if *Don Juan* works. Moreover, *Don Juan* will tell us quite a lot about why we now think as we do. The curious thing is that *Don Juan* now appears to be read more easily than any other long poem in English and continues to grow in popularity. Perhaps we should not underestimate its capacity to educate us in the proper conduct of verse.

Comedy

What sort of poem is *Don Juan* and what, if anything, is its major concern? Different answers have been given to these questions and some have argued that they cannot be answered at all because the poem is like a ragbag or a holdall that will contain anything that Byron chooses to put into it.

It is true that any account of the poem cannot ignore or argue away its diversity and apparent randomness, but my own view is that *Don Juan* is as much a particular kind of poem as Milton's *Paradise Lost* or Wordsworth's *The Prelude* and that it has clear concerns that can be confidently identified. The title of this section indicates what this form and these concerns might be.

We have seen that it is very hard to isolate themes in *Don Juan*, such as love, because they are connected with one another, with the archetypal story of Adam and Eve's Fall – which Byron consistently refers to and thinks through – and with politics, psychology and much else beside. However, the union of individual and social, natural and sophisticated, random and providential forms of life is itself characteristic of many kinds of comedy including Shakespeare's. Byron's long poem is not a play, of course, and it is only the happy conclusion of a comedy that firmly establishes its character. Byron's poem, on the other hand, is unfinished. In many ways too, as we have seen, *Don Juan* is like an epic poem in its scale, a romance in its adventure, satire in its indignation, and the novel in its concern with the interactions of individual and social life. It may seem pointless to insist that it is, despite all this, a comedy. Yet we must do so. For what we have to take most seriously in *Don Juan* is the forward momentum of the poem and the connection of its parts. Insofar as we do this, we are assuming the poem to have a particular sort of life and we are assuming too that the momentum and energies of the poem in some way represent and give us some sense of a larger world than the poem itself. Byron makes this point for us in an apparently whimsical way in that important section introducing the first ghost story in Canto XVI, which we have already noticed:

> And therefore mortals, cavil not at all.
>   Believe. If 'tis improbable, you must,
> And if it is impossible, you shall.
>   'Tis always best to take things upon trust.
>
> (XVI, 6)

He is talking here about believing ghost stories, believing Byron's own poem, and religious belief. These things are not identical and Byron's tongue is in his cheek, but he is quite serious in his recommendation. We will, in fact, believe the ghost story that he is about to tell us, it will be true in the poem (and out of it if there is a ghost in Newstead Abbey), and by trusting it we will be taken through to the eventual unmasking of the Duchess of Fitz-Fulke as the second ghost and so to laughter and renewed confidence in the poem's capacity to surprise us as life does.

Comedies, in general, tell us that ' 'Tis always best to take things upon trust' like this because in comedy everything works towards a just and happy conclusion whatever the odds against it. What we are finally given is always better than what we have lost and all previous trials and disappointments seem, from the standpoint of comedy's final scene, to be vindicated as the necessary means by which the best of all outcomes has been reached.

How seriously we take all this will depend upon whether we think that the form of comedy is corroborated and upheld by energies inherent in life itself and its unknowable resources ('Nature', 'Providence', 'God') or whether we think that comedy is simply a fiction designed to cheer us up and make us momentarily forget the unpalatable truth that the universe we live in is randomly organized and wholly indifferent to human welfare. Comedies will become more 'serious' in this latter view if they hint at this bleak state of affairs and thus become 'problem', 'dark' or even 'black' comedies. Some critics have argued that *Don Juan* does propose such a dark view and have quoted this or that line to support their case. What we ought to consider, however, is the whole shape and momentum of the poem, how it reconciles us to loss, if it does so, and what, if anything, we finally gain.

We have examined all the episodes in the poem in some detail. What are they concerned with and what can we learn from their sequence? Can we say that they all form part of a comic pattern?

It is clear first of all that the episodes in Seville, Haidée's Isle, the Harem, Catherine's Court and even Norman Abbey centre in their love-narratives. The other two episodes, the Shipwreck and the Siege, are accounts of destruction and death. Finally, the account of Juan's travels from Russia to London (Cantos X–XII) has no clear narrative concern at all. Set out like this, it looks as though the poem is mainly concerned with the adventures, especially love-adventures, of Don Juan. Some narratives of love tell a single story, such as Manzoni's *The Betrothed*, but this can only be done by interposing all kinds of obstacles to the eventual union of the couple. Where a narrative is made up of a number of love-stories, like *Don Juan*, it will typically be found in four patterns. These are repetition, survival, decline or ascent. This will need some explanation. If, for instance, we read a pornographic novel (perhaps we should not) such as John Cleland's *Fanny Hill*, the basic form of the narrative can be no other than a repetition, however artfully varied, of the same privileged activity. If on the other hand we read a picaresque novel like Defoe's *Moll Flanders*, we are mainly interested in the sheer survival of the heroine rather than in her numerous love-affairs as such. Other love-narratives may readily arrange themselves into a declining sequence. Such is the progress of any rake; the fate of any Cressida. Conversely, love may be pictured as a steady ascent where Romeo forgets Rosaline and finds Juliet, or Dante loses Beatrice only to locate her for ever in *Paradiso*, or Leontes (in *The Winter's Tale*) loses one Hermione and gains another. As this last example suggests, ascent may be a form of loss and restoration where what is restored is greater than, though in some respects identical with, what was taken away.

All these patterns are found in *Don Juan* and, in a way, compete with one another, but they are not equally valid. The original Don Juan story is, of course, made up of repeated seductions and a judgement. The judgement is appropriate because the whole character of the villain-hero's life is given to us in his repeated acts of sexual violation. Byron's Don Juan never seduces anyone, but the story is conducted through a series of love-episodes, each of which culminates in consummation. Thus as soon as Julia and Juan make love, the narrator cuts abruptly to several months later (I, 121) when Alfonso is to catch them together and the affair ends. Similarly, as soon as the narrator can say 'And now 'twas done' of Juan and Haidée (II, 204), we cut to the arrival of Lambro, who is to disengage them. In the next episode Juan sleeps with Dudù once, the Sultana moves to separate them and we cut to the siege. Only with Catherine the Great do we have no sense of a specific first occasion of love-making. This is because love here is presented as a task and, of course, Juan falls sick. At the end of the poem we trace the movement from dinner to midnight that leads up to Fitz-Fulke's seduction, if successful, of Juan. In all these cases Byron never attempts to fill in the psychological details or emotional upsets of these love-affairs. A couple is formed, a couple is sundered. That is all. Similarly, Juan's seduction is always accomplished simply by finding an attractive woman presenting herself immediately in front of him, as Fitz-Fulke does at the end of Canto XVI. There are no snatched or elaborately planned meetings, no hidden letters, no misunderstandings or reconciliations. The pattern is simple and it is the same throughout the poem. In this sense Byron's Juan reveals himself, as any Don Juan does, through a simple repeated set of circumstances. Moreover, he seems to have no links with the future or the past. If others plan a future for him, a shipwreck intervenes and takes him to a woman. If he is given a love-letter to remember someone by, sea-sickness will confound his attempted attention to it. He lives always in the present and the present will always bring him to an agreeable bed-partner.

As this might suggest, Juan is thus a survivor as well as one who finds himself repeating the same pattern in different circumstances. Of the 'forty thousand' who had manned the wall in Ismail, there are left only 'some hundreds' (VIII, 127); but we may be sure that Juan will survive, just as he, alone, survives the shipwreck of the *Trinidada* in Canto II. Juan is indeed the epitome of the one who survives any mimic death that assails him. When rescued from the sea in Canto II, he sleeps 'like the dead'. He is 'half-killed' and 'weak' as he sails past the tombs of dead Greek heroes and leaves the corpse of Haidée behind him. When surfeited with Catherine, he 'grew sick' and his condition 'augured of the dead'. In each case he revives to new life. When he first sees the ghost of Norman Abbey, he becomes 'cold and silent' and 'Something like illness' weighs on his spirit, although of course the second ghost who is really the frisky young Duchess makes his veins 'no longer cold, but heated'. In the last lines of the poem, however, the morning after this occurrence finds him 'wan and worn'.

Against these patterns of repetition and survival we may set out the evidence for Juan's decline. In Canto X the narrator tells us this clearly enough:

> About this time, as might have been anticipated,
>   Seduced by youth and dangerous examples,
> Don Juan grew, I fear, a little dissipated,
>
>   (X, 23)

We have suspected this, however, since the siege, where Juan 'had shone in the late slaughter' (IX, 29). The pairing of Juan with Leila, the little orphan girl whom he rescued, seems to symbolize the innocence he has lost. In England too Juan shines in the society that the narrator castigates, for he was 'all things unto people of all sorts' (XIV, 31), listened 'to the topics most in vogue' and only smiled at all this 'in secret — cunning rogue' (XIV, 37). By Canto XVI the narrator can say that Juan 'had lately lost/Or hardened' his capacity for 'some feelings' (XVI, 107).

There remains the pattern of ascent. However, before we consider this, we should assemble some of the facts that do not fit in with the three readings of narrative pattern that we have set out.

A repetition pattern can never quite be what it appears. Pornography is instantly arresting but ultimately boring and ridiculous as well. A routine of intensity yields neither the satisfactions of habit nor the required ecstasies. The attempt to repeat intensity at all costs leads to dullness, loathing or mirth. The original Don Juan suddenly finds himself not in the chosen dangers of a violated bed but in the hell prepared for violators, and the audience relishes the new intensity brought about by the end of Juan's repeated escapades. In the old play Don Juan's comic servant warns his master of this conclusion. In Byron's poem the narrator is much more prominent in his interjections which, though spirited in themselves, emphasize the brevity of youth's pleasures and the uncertainty of human affairs and knowledge. Hence we cannot simply accept the repetition of love's pleasures as sufficient.

Juan's survival too, though important, is not interesting in itself. *Don Juan* is only superficially like a picaresque novel because we are never directed to the mechanisms of survival as such. When, for instance, Juan survives starvation in an open boat, we are not told how he does it. On the contrary he does not try to survive by the cannibalistic methods used by the others. Picaresque heroes and heroines learn to live by their wits and make us interested in the low-life world that always survives like this. Don Juan, however, remains a noble, pairs with the privileged (even Haidée is a 'princess of her father's land') and survives through good luck and kind fortune. His battle decorations (VIII, 140) are appropriate, for he is indeed as much a hero as an anti-hero. A true picaresque hero would be more likely to survive by deserting. Indeed, the pattern of apparent death and resurrection to love that marks Juan's adventures, as we have seen, does not belong to the world of mundane survival or scrutinized experience at all. Juan is an emblem of love's force. If he survives, he does so because something acts in and through him. His ordinary life is larger than life.

So the suggestion that Juan has declined into a particularly accomplished house guest in England who joins in an ordinary, if aristocratic, social world is a deeply worrying one. But not all the evidence supports this either. Leila, for example, an untainted presence in the poem, is eventually given into the custody of a Lady Pinchbeck (XI, 41–51) who is presented as experienced and gentle. She is a much better guide to Leila's youth, of which she is the 'mild reprover', than anyone young Juan found in Seville. Yet Lady Pinchbeck likes Juan:

> Because she thought him a good heart at bottom,
> A little spoilt, but not so altogether.
>
> (XII, 49)

This makes it quite clear that we are not supposed to see Juan's progress as simply one from innocence to experience. The poem has necessarily presented us with this pattern as Juan travels from one woman to another, but Byron is more interested in whether and how something untainted can be kept alive or renewed in Juan than with recording the taintings of his hero. If Juan were to become the lover of Lady Adeline, without too much fuss and at her instigation, then he would have declined into a gigolo or rake. Instead of this he is drawn towards Aurora Raby who, alone in Norman Abbey, can prevent such a decline and who

> had renewed
> In him some feelings he had lately lost
> (XVI, 107)

This is the only time in the poem (if we except his rescue of Leila) that Juan moves towards a woman, as opposed to being pursued by one. It appears as an instinctive recognition on his part and confirms the truth of Lady Pinchbeck's observation that, despite everything, he retains 'a good heart'. But what is Juan drawn towards? There are two possible paths to take here and we must choose between them.

The first possibility is that Juan is drawn here, as always, by a Romantic ideal of love that he sometimes attains, especially in Haidée, but which he invariably loses and again yearns for. Aurora Raby, in this view, is another version of the same ideal and she will be lost in the same way. Many Romantic poems, such as Keats's *Endymion* and Shelley's *Alastor*, trace a similar pattern and, if we continue the quotation given above (XVI, 107) into the next stanzas, Byron does seem to be saying something quite like this. Some critics, especially those familiar with Romantic stereotypes present Don Juan in this way, although if we look more closely we will be led along a different path.

It is very important, certainly, that Aurora recalls Haidée both to Juan and to the reader (XV, 58). This is the clearest indication in the entire poem that Byron has in mind a single focus for all Juan's escapades and that the poem is not, as musicians say, simply 'through-composed' but can recapitulate its themes. But it is equally important that Aurora resembles 'not his lost Haidée' for Haidée

> Was Nature's all. Aurora could not be
> Nor would be thus
>
>>> (XV, 58)

Aurora is less 'warm' than Haidée but as 'lovely', as 'radiant', and she knows more. She is both innocent and wise. She is wise in the straightforward sense that she 'looked more on books than faces' (XV, 85) and in this is the exact opposite of Haidée, who looked at Juan's face

> And read (the only book she could) the lines
> Of his fair face . . .
>
>>> (II, 162)

In looking at Juan's face thus, Haidée, even though she is 'devout as well as fair' (II, 193), forgets what she knows about the Fall of man and the consequent impossibility of recovering a lasting paradise in Juan's face. Aurora, on the other hand, looked

> as if she sat by Eden's door
> And grieved for those who could return no more.
>
>>> (XV, 45)

Aurora therefore is in touch with some force outside herself (like Haidée's 'Nature') that makes her vibrant and innocent, hence attractive to Juan, yet she knows and never forgets, as Haidée does, the character of fallen human experience. It is for this reason that Aurora not only 'could not' be like Haidée but also 'Nor would be thus'. It is hard to see how Aurora could be destroyed or lost in the way that Haidée was, for she has already taken into herself the knowledge and the death that do away with Haidée. She cannot therefore be a repeat version of what was glimpsed in Haidée, whose destiny is to be grasped and lost yet again. There can be no doubt of this, for Byron's indications are very precise, but the explicitly religious ideas that are now in play may seem out of place in *Don Juan*. Byron already sprang one surprise on us at the outset of the poem by making his Juan seduced rather than seducing; now, at the end of it, he appears to be praising virginity and even holiness in a poem that has, apparently, been in love with Nature's turbulent and uncontrollable energies. Yet the whole character of the poem is more clearly given to us in this movement than by anything else.

Don Juan is not a novel. It is not about 'character' or 'what happens'. It is about life's energies and whether we can trust to them. The poem itself comes as close as words can to representing those energies to us, both as they are in themselves and as art represents, shapes and fictionalizes them. The first half of the poem, despite the narrator's interventions, makes us side with Juan and follow not so much his story as the renewal, canto by canto, in always differing circumstances of the same energies and their fulfilment in him. The reader's attention to this sequence is like that of a comedy because we learn that things will turn out well despite all the odds against happy outcomes. As we learn to 'take things upon trust' in this way, we are directed partly to the apparently inexhaustible creativity of the writer of the poem who can, it seems, cope with anything and partly to Juan himself. Juan does not simply survive in the poem: he awakes from a series of apparent deaths or end-points to fresh life with a new heroine. We are directed, therefore, both to a trust in the energies that underlie Juan's life in themselves and to a confidence that these energies will always shape themselves into a repeated comic cadence. The poem lives through a series of happy-ever-after endings, interrupted by some disaster that is never allowed to settle into a tragic or pathetic shape but itself sets in motion a resumption of the original comic pattern as though it had never been displaced.

This is an entirely original, yet recognizably comic structure, but it cannot be employed indefinitely. The poem gives us the satisfaction of endless and energetic processes and yet it also gives us the sense of implied cadence. It is formless and yet it is presented in well-marked and wonderfully balanced episodes. Byron prevents this formula from becoming wearisome by varying and intensifying the obstacles to comic renewal in the poem. The greatest of these are the Siege and Catherine the Great (Cantos VII–X), which block the middle of the poem and force it to change character. This is because the energies of war in the Siege seem far too close to love's energies for comfort and the unacceptable cadence of Catherine after Ismail makes this connection horribly explicit to us. This takes away all our confidence in the repeated formulas of the poem and, so it seems, of life itself.

The second half of the poem, therefore, is dominated by the narrator. For example, his digressions take up one quarter of the stanzas in the first eight cantos but require almost half the space in the next seven. Love disappears from the poem as does unexpected incident, for we have lost confidence in both.

This, surely, is why Byron writes Aurora Raby into the end of the poem. All the evidence is that she did not form part of his original conception of the English cantos. She is a religiously conceived figure who knows all about the Fall and seems to be in touch with something like divine grace rather than with Nature. Or rather, the 'Nature' of Norman Abbey that is in harmony with the ruins of the old building seems to be bound up with transcendent powers as well as with natural life. Yet Aurora Raby functions as a heroine in the poem even, so it seems, as a potential wife for Juan. At exactly the same point as Aurora's entrance into *Don Juan*, the narrator starts digressing much less. In Canto XVI less than a quarter of the stanzas are digressive. Similarly, unexpected incidents (the two ghost stories) revive the narrative of the poem, which has virtually disappeared since Catherine the Great. The final surprise of the poem is the reappearance of sex, linked again with laughter and surprise, in the blonde Duchess disguised as a ghostly Black Friar at the end of Canto XVI.

All of this must mean that Byron can only see his way to the use of his old formulas and the old confidence in love and life's energies by creating a new kind of heroine who, in a sense, represents an ascent from Haidée and all the other heroines and yet, in another way, restores these to us. That is why Byron is at such pains to mark both the connection and the difference between Haidée and Aurora. But why is a religious language so necessary to him at this point?

We have seen throughout this study of Byron's poetry that he is always at least as serious about religion as he is about politics, literature or human love. The competing claims of all these were particularly concentrated during his last months in Italy while he was writing the last cantos of *Don Juan*. Should he stay with his mistress Teresa, Countess

Guiccioli, become a Catholic, go to America or help the Greeks in their struggle for independence? And what was still owing to *Don Juan* which, he knew very well, was his greatest poem? Nevertheless we do not need to speculate about Byron's own dilemma. *Don Juan* itself, and some reflection about the nature of comedy, should allow us to frame a sufficient answer to our question.

What we are shown in the Siege of Ismail and in Catherine the Great's indifference to death is a horrifying version of what *Don Juan* lives to celebrate. It is not that we cannot trust life's energies here, but that these energies, incarnated in Catherine the Great, seem wholly indifferent to human concerns and coincide with human feelings only insofar as life's sole aim is its own purposeless self-renewal. After rushing Juan from a battle-field where thousands of soldiers die to a bed where, apparently, hundreds of soldiers labour for Catherine's unappeasable satisfaction, it is impossible that we should again respond with enthusiasm to a scene such as Haidée's bringing Juan back to life in Canto I I. For it is not only Haidée who thus reawakens Juan, it is also life and Nature operating through her. Haidée lives out one part of the cycle (death to life) in her brief idyll with Juan, although she encounters the other part (life to death) in her dream in Canto I V and in the death, as she thinks, of Juan. Unlike Catherine she cannot remain indifferent to this and dies of the intolerable connections that she has discovered. What destroys Haidée is the foundation of Catherine's being.

It would be impossible for the poem to claim suddenly that none of this has happened or that it makes no difference because the very agency upon which the poem relies for recovery (life always begins again) has been exposed as inhuman and pointless in Cantos V I I–X. Consequently, if the poem is not to settle into complete cynicism and despair about the life that it proposes for celebration, it will have to seek out a source of energy that yet remains untainted, whatever appearances such as Catherine's may suggest. A religious reading of life is the only real candidate here, for nearly all religions characteristically presuppose that the world is tainted but that it proceeds from, and still obscurely represents, its untainted origins in God. Greek, Roman and European comedy often activate religious resonances; Shakespeare does so constantly, in order to make us affirm the validity, and not merely the fictional advantage, of comic conclusion.

Throughout Byron's writings we often find an explicitly religious diagnosis of human life. The abbot in *Manfred*, for instance, tells

Manfred that he understands all about sin and the necessity for redemption but will not accept the corresponding Christian cure. Aurora Raby who, unlike the tragic Manfred, lives in a comic poem, is the closest Byron ever comes to endorsing the cure as well as the diagnosis.

We can point to two interrelated features of Aurora here that should clarify this and help us to a conclusion. The first is Byron's repeated emphasis on Aurora's connection with a world beyond this tainted one of our immediate apprehension. She has 'an aspect beyond time' and is 'Apart from the surrounding world' (XV, 45, 47). Again, 'The worlds beyond this world's perplexing waste/Had more of her existence' (XVI, 48). But it is important to note that she is beautiful and present within and not beyond 'this world's perplexing waste' herself. She is far more substantial, for example, than Lady Adeline, who, in the customary view, lives in the 'real world' from which Aurora has withdrawn. This could present a real difficulty for Byron because the stunning, immediate presence of his heroines has been insisted upon and is, in effect, what seduces and renews Juan. How can Aurora compete with them in present attractiveness while, at the same time, remaining in touch with something more than the flow of natural life? Byron has one stanza in particular that deftly resolves this difficulty. In this stanza he explains that Juan blushes when he catches Aurora's eye on his. Aurora, however, 'did not blush in turn' (XVI, 94). This is much odder and more specific than it might seem. Julia, Haidée, Dudù and the Sultana engage Juan by an exactly rendered interplay of blushing and palpitation that Byron always calls 'glow' and, as we have seen, often relates to sunsets. He realizes in this way the connections between human relationships, individual consciousness and physical life. It is easy to see, therefore, why Aurora does not blush like this. She is not wholly an emblem of natural life. But is she pallid and 'cold' as Lady Adeline jealously insists (XV, 49)? Byron writes four lines in the stanza to suggest a wonderfully different perspective:

> Yet grew a little pale. With what? Concern?
>   I know not, but her colour ne'er was high,
> Though sometimes faintly flushed and always clear,
> As deep seas in a sunny atmosphere.

> (XVI, 94)

Aurora, it appears from these exactly stated lines, has a kind of warmth ('faintly flushed'); this is caused not by her own immediate, physical life but by a reflection of sources of life that exist in a different dimension, just as the depths of the sea catch the colour of the sun that exists in another world from them. The condition of this receptivity, for both seas and Aurora is to be 'always clear'. Aurora does not place any obstacle to the activity of another source of light and warmth within her. Hence she does not glow with her own life but shines with some altogether different life. Her 'bright . . . large dark eyes' turn 'unto the stars for loftier rays' and 'Sadly shone, as seraphs shine'. In this way Byron restores an irresistible female presence to his poem, but she is untainted, cannot become tainted, and therefore allows us to 'take things upon trust again'. So much so that the very physical glow of Fitz-Fulke, scarcely free from the world's taint, is acceptable too. Byron, however, allows us to feel this at the end of Canto XVI but then have our doubts at the beginning of Canto XVII.

What happens at the end of the poem, then, is an extraordinary restoration of its comic mode, overthrown earlier, by the unmistakable suggestion of a religious reading of life that accepts the fallen nature of experience but grounds its hope elsewhere. This operates alongside the ordinary social world in which we live (daytime Norman Abbey) and is in tension with, though not outright opposition to, the mischievous imperatives of the flesh (Fitz-Fulke). The patterning here is almost like that of an allegory. There is nothing else like it in English poetry, though Shelley's *The Triumph of Life* and Keats's *Fall of Hyperion* offer some parallels. Byron manages to think clearly and deeply while at the same time preserving lightness of touch and considerable pace right to the 'end' of his poem.

We have spent some time with *Don Juan*'s conclusion because this, more clearly than anything else, shows us that Byron does not write at random or allow his poem to meander into any territory that it chooses. Without the last two cantos we might perhaps say that *Don Juan* begins as a romance and ends as a satirical novel. With the last two cantos it is quite clear that, whatever happens, Byron is at pains to maintain *Don Juan* as a poem whose prevailing mode is that of comedy.

Conclusion: Attitudes to Byron

When we read a poet's works, even if they are new to us and we know little or nothing about the poet, we cannot avoid picking up the received attitudes to his work. 'Byronic', for example, is an epithet that is used by many who have never read a line of Byron himself. It is best, therefore, to have some idea of what these attitudes are, so that our own discrimination is allowed more scope. The history of Byron's reputation tells us a great deal about the history of English poetry and taste in the last two hundred years.

Byron was immensely famous from 1812 onwards. His poems sold in unprecedentedly large quantities and were translated almost immediately into most European languages. His fame was built especially upon *Childe Harold*, the Oriental tales, *Manfred* and *Cain*. The note of defiance and the stance of the Byronic hero were, accordingly, central to these early reactions to Byron. Melancholy, Satanic defiance of authority and, consequently, sympathy for rebellion, sexual passion and liberty made Byron's poetry fashionable in a world of revolutionary and liberal sentiment. His feeling for history and sympathetic depiction of exotic, semi-feudal societies, on the other hand, fitted in with the equally strong movements of conservative revival. His poetry was not read very carefully, for the most part. It was read for its energy and the Romantic stances that it seemed to authorize and give definition to. This image of Byron persists, especially on the Continent, where it became bound up with revolutionary aspiration, nationalist sentiment and liberal opinion.

In England, however, a reaction against Byron's poetry was soon under way. Byron himself sensed this while writing *Don Juan*, which was, with some significant exceptions, little read and widely disliked. Victorian taste stabilized into a decidedly Romantic form that left little room for Byron. Coleridge, Keats and Shelley were seen as more poetic (that is, more intensely lyrical) and Wordsworth was seen as wiser (that is more positive) than Byron. Thomas Carlyle in *Sartor Resartus* (1836) advised his readers to 'Close thy Byron: open thy Goethe' and Victorian readers obliged by closing their Byrons and opening their Wordsworths. Byron was patronized as a powerful but crude force, easy to understand, and not a very sound influence on life or literature.

There were powerful voices (Ruskin, even Arnold) saying something rather different, but this view of Byron persisted and still influences the half informed. It went hand and glove with the next phase of Byron readership.

After the First World War, literature, music, ballet, painting and architecture were transformed by spectacular reactions to what was then considered to be Romantic and nineteenth-century taste. As we look back on Stravinsky, Picasso, Joyce, Eliot and others from a position nearer to the twenty-first century than to the nineteenth, many of these 'modernist' ideas and forms seem to belong far more to what preceded than to what followed them. At the time, however, anything that was anti-Romantic or anti-Victorian was considered a good thing by those in the know. The opposite of a Romantic lyric by Shelley was a metaphysical lyric by Donne, hence Shelley was closed and Donne was opened. The opposite to a long Romantic poem or to that Victorian touchstone *Paradise Lost* was a satire by Pope or Dryden, so the latter were elevated above the former. Byron presented these revaluers with a special case. He was the quintessential Romantic poet and revered as such by all of Europe. Yet the Victorians had downgraded him and, in particular, had belittled *Don Juan* and ignored *The Vision of Judgement*. Hence a new assessment could be made. Victorian judgement of Byron's 'Romantic' poems was largely preserved. They were still considered to be crude, rhetorical and overstated. On the other hand *Don Juan* and *The Vision of Judgement* were 'satires' that could be celebrated as forerunners of the English satirical poetry of the Thirties.

This British view of Byron influenced most major works of criticism written from the Thirties to the Fifties and still controls the educational syllabuses which, in their turn, shape this book. It has, however, long since run out of steam. No new view has clearly displaced it. However, the profoundly imaginative, if slightly eccentric, criticism of G. Wilson Knight from the Thirties onwards and a spate of books by American critics in the Sixties and Seventies have completely altered the picture. All of these take *Don Juan* and most of Byron's other poems with complete seriousness. His political plays in particular have been systematically praised for their intelligence and *The Island* is now seen as one of Byron's major achievements. These critics have been influenced, of course, by our renewed sensitivity to and respect for the myths, inherited antitheses and structural patterns that underlie all poetry and, manifestly, are the life of Byron's verse. There is no consensus beyond this. As always, some critics emphasize Byron's optimism, others his bitter nihilism. There is now much more importance attached to the religious frame of Byron's imagination, but some still regard him as an enlightened forerunner of atheistic relativism and so on. His relationship with the other Romantics, often attempted, has never been satisfactorily formulated.

All this has been overtaken in the late Seventies and Eighties by the rise and setting, though not the extinction, of the cult of literary theory (Structuralism and Post-Structuralism) and a marked decline in public confidence in, and familiarity with, all forms of literature. It is easy to see how previous forms of criticism that were so much concerned with structures, myths, symbols and narrative patterns could, if persisted in, dissolve away any clear sense of real authors or real historical worlds that exist apart from fictions that can be endlessly interpreted. This is why so little resistance was offered to the new dogma. In the now received view of literature in general, there is no real distinction between Byron and 'Byron'. Both are made up by words and neither exist when we are not talking about them. Anyone who has read *Don Juan* with attention will know that such an opinion is hard to controvert, contains some truth, and is quite crazy. The distant origins of ideas like these are undoubtedly contained within the origins of Romanticism itself. Byron can be seen to have anticipated and pilloried the ultimate logic of those Romantic tendencies in his contemporaries that seem to underlie such modern cults of fictionality and meaningful meaninglessness at the outset. *Don Juan* is pitched exactly at that midway point between absurdity, mystery and good sense that the imagination may occupy and illumine but cannot claim to have created or to regulate.

There are signs here and there that Byron's bid to influence the future development of English and European culture in other ways than that suggested by 'Byronic' may, even now, have surprising force. It took a century and a half before he was allowed a memorial in Westminster Abbey. Byron's life and writings still form unexhausted parts of English and European history and summon us to a fresh understanding of what we have forgotten, gained and remain painfully conscious of in that history.

Further Reading

Selections

Penguin Poetry Library: *Byron*. Poems selected by A. S. B. Glover (reissued 1985). Cheap and handy but very restricted.

The Oxford Authors: *Byron*. Edited by J. McGann (1986). An excellent selection including complete *Childe Harold*, *Don Juan* and some letters.

Complete Poems

It is always best to buy a complete Byron if possible. The Oxford Standard Authors edition is the best available. There are many second-hand editions that can be cheaply purchased.

Letters

Lord Byron: Selected Letters and Journals. Edited by Peter Gunn (Penguin, reissued 1984).

Biography

Leslie Marchand, *Byron: A Portrait* (John Murray, 1971; Futura paperback, 1976). A superb biography.

Criticism

M. K. Joseph, *Byron the Poet* (London, 1964). The best general introduction to Byron's poetry.

Bernard Beatty, *Byron's Don Juan* (Croom Helm, 1985). Tries to establish by detailed argument and close reading the cogency of the interpretation of *Don Juan* found in this Masterstudy.

FOR THE BEST IN PAPERBACKS, LOOK FOR THE

In every corner of the world, on every subject under the sun, Penguin represents quality and variety – the very best in publishing today.

For complete information about books available from Penguin – including Pelicans, Puffins, Peregrines and Penguin Classics – and how to order them, write to us at the appropriate address below. Please note that for copyright reasons the selection of books varies from country to country.

In the United Kingdom: For a complete list of books available from Penguin in the U.K., please write to *Dept E.P., Penguin Books Ltd, Harmondsworth, Middlesex, UB7 0DA*

In the United States: For a complete list of books available from Penguin in the U.S., please write to *Dept BA, Penguin, 299 Murray Hill Parkway, East Rutherford, New Jersey 07073*

In Canada: For a complete list of books available from Penguin in Canada, please write to *Penguin Books Canada Ltd, 2801 John Street, Markham, Ontario L3R 1B4*

In Australia: For a complete list of books available from Penguin in Australia, please write to the *Marketing Department, Penguin Books Australia Ltd, P.O. Box 257, Ringwood, Victoria 3134*

In New Zealand: For a complete list of books available from Penguin in New Zealand, please write to the *Marketing Department, Penguin Books (NZ) Ltd, Private Bag, Takapuna, Auckland 9*

In India: For a complete list of books available from Penguin, please write to *Penguin Overseas Ltd, 706 Eros Apartments, 56 Nehru Place, New Delhi, 110019*

In Holland: For a complete list of books available from Penguin in Holland, please write to *Penguin Books Nederland B.V., Postbus 195, NL–1380AD Weesp, Netherlands*

In Germany: For a complete list of books available from Penguin, please write to *Penguin Books Ltd, Friedrichstrasse 10 – 12, D–6000 Frankfurt Main 1, Federal Republic of Germany*

In Spain: For a complete list of books available from Penguin in Spain, please write to *Longman Penguin España, Calle San Nicolas 15, E–28013 Madrid, Spain*

PENGUIN CLASSICS

Netochka Nezvanova   Fyodor Dostoyevsky

Dostoyevsky's first book tells the story of 'Nameless Nobody' and introduces many of the themes and issues which will dominate his great
masterpieces.

Selections from the Carmina Burana   A verse translation by David Parlett

The famous songs from the *Carmina Burana* (made into an oratorio by
Carl Orff) tell of lecherous monks and corrupt clerics, drinkers and
gamblers, and the fleeting pleasures of youth.

Fear and Trembling   Søren Kierkegaard

A profound meditation on the nature of faith and submission to God's will
which examines with startling originality the story of Abraham and Isaac.

Selected Prose   Charles Lamb

Lamb's famous essays (under the strange pseudonym of Elia) on anything
and everything have long been celebrated for their apparently innocent
charm; this major new edition allows readers to discover the darker and
more interesting aspects of Lamb.

The Picture of Dorian Gray   Oscar Wilde

Wilde's superb and macabre novella, one of his supreme works, is
reprinted here with a masterly Introduction and valuable Notes by Peter
Ackroyd.

A Treatise of Human Nature   David Hume

A universally acknowledged masterpiece by 'the greatest of all British
Philosophers' – A. J. Ayer

PENGUIN CLASSICS

A Passage to India   E. M. Forster

Centred on the unresolved mystery in the Marabar Caves, Forster's great work provides the definitive evocation of the British Raj.

The Republic   Plato

The best-known of Plato's dialogues, *The Republic* is also one of the supreme masterpieces of Western philosophy whose influence cannot be overestimated.

The Life of Johnson   James Boswell

Perhaps the finest 'life' ever written, Boswell's *Johnson* captures for all time one of the most colourful and talented figures in English literary history.

Remembrance of Things Past (3 volumes)   Marcel Proust

This revised version by Terence Kilmartin of C. K. Scott Moncrieff's original translation has been universally acclaimed – available for the first time in paperback.

Metamorphoses   Ovid

A golden treasury of myths and legends which has proved a major influence on Western literature.

A Nietzsche Reader   Friedrich Nietzsche

A superb selection from all the major works of one of the greatest thinkers and writers in world literature, translated into clear, modern English.

FOR THE BEST IN PAPERBACKS, LOOK FOR THE 🐧

PENGUIN MASTERSTUDIES

This comprehensive list, designed to help advanced level and first-year undergraduate studies, includes:

SUBJECTS
Applied Mathematics
Biology
Drama: Text into Performance
Geography
Pure Mathematics

LITERATURE
Dr Faustus
Eugénie Grandet
The Great Gatsby
The Mill on the Floss
A Passage to India
Persuasion
Portrait of a Lady
Tender Is the Night
Vanity Fair
The Waste Land

CHAUCER
The Knight's Tale
The Miller's Tale
The Nun's Priest's Tale
The Pardoner's Tale
The Prologue to The Canterbury
    Tales
A Chaucer Handbook

SHAKESPEARE
Hamlet
King Lear
Measure for Measure
Othello
The Tempest
A Shakespeare Handbook

'Standing somewhere between the literal, word-by-word explication of more usual notes and the abstractions of an academic monograph, the Masterstudies series is an admirable introduction to mainstream literary criticism for A Level students, in particular for those contemplating reading English at university. More than that, it is also a model of what student notes can achieve' – *The Times Literary Supplement*